PORTIA

PORTIA

The Life of
Portia Washington Pittman
the Daughter of
Booker T. Washington

RUTH ANN STEWART

Doubleday & Company, Inc.
Garden City, New York
1977

B
Pit

Library of Congress Cataloging in Publication Data

Stewart, Ruth Ann.
Portia.

Bibliography: p. 144.
Includes index.
1. Pittman, Portia Washington, 1883–
2. Washington, Booker Taliaferro, 1859?–1915.
I. Title.
E185.97.P595S83   301.45′19′6073024 [B]
ISBN: 0-385-05329-0
Library of Congress Catalog Card Number 75–6167

11721

TO
Ann Mitchell Stewart
and
Elmer A. Stewart

Contents

Preface

Portia Washington Pittman is a woman, a black American, and the survivor of nearly one hundred years of a tumultuous personal and public history. From its beginning, when she was born the first child and only daughter of Booker T. Washington, her life was marked by the extraordinary. Booker T. Washington was a man who in his lifetime came to control the political, economic, and social destiny of black America to such an extent that even today, sixty years after his death, his name still calls forth controversy. Born a slave in 1856, Washington scaled the heights of fame and power through his founding in Alabama of one of the first private training schools for black men and women, Tuskegee Institute. From this base, the "Wizard of Tuskegee" preached a doctrine of social separatism and race uplift through physical labor, which found fertile ground in the post-Reconstruction South. Andrew Carnegie, John D. Rockefeller, and other representatives of moneyed northern interests flocked to his support, anointing him "race leader" and the Moses of his people. Presidents and colonial powers abroad sought his council on his seemingly successful solution to the containment of the race problem. But in other quarters, Washington was roundly condemned for his non-integrationist, anti-intellectual posture, particularly by the Harvard-educated black scholar W. E. B. Du Bois and the interracial founders of the emerging civil rights organization, the National Association for the Advancement of Colored People (NAACP). Washington was denounced in print and from the podium but, even his critics would admit, was seldom outmaneuvered.

Portia could not grow up immune to the controversy surrounding her famous father—was he savior or Uncle Tom? But hers was to be a sheltered, comfortable life until as an adult woman she made a conscious choice to charge into the very eye of the storm. For the first quarter of her long life, Portia was a living contradiction to the Washington doctrine. Left motherless while still an infant, she was pampered and prepared for education as the only black at a series of New England private schools, graduating from Bradford Academy (now Bradford College), Massachusetts, with a degree in music in 1905. A promising pianist, she was sent to Berlin to study with a student of Franz Liszt where she eagerly embraced the gay bohemian student life. Family pressure and a sense of obligation to what she considered her special heritage combined to bring her home to marry Sidney Pittman, a brilliant but eccentric architect and the father of her three children. Her father's premature death in 1915 and a painful breakup of her marriage and family left Portia a woman alone in what was to become an endless struggle for personal dignity, artistic fulfillment, and vindication of the Washington name.

Despite the vicissitudes which marked that struggle, Portia's adventurous spirit, philosophical outlook, and hardy sense of humor had sustained her into a graceful old age of nearly ninety years when I first had the good fortune of meeting her at her home in Washington, D.C. A woman of great warmth, she talked easily and openly through repeated interviews, which were marked as much by her concern for the comfort of the author as her interest in having the de-

tails of her life recorded. She would begin these sessions
seated with her ankles crossed and hands demurely folded
in her lap after the manner instilled in her by her proper
Victorian upbringing. As she warmed to her subject, resur-
recting long-ago occurrences with a vivacity and recall that
were both informative and enthralling, the high spirit which
had propelled her through her long life could not be denied.
With a sprinkling of pithy German phrases mastered in her
student days or an animated rendering of her father's in-
famous Atlanta speech, she would quit her proper repose
for a rousing session at her old upright piano. With gracious good humor and to the gratitude of those of us of a
younger generation, Portia Washington Pittman has reflected
on her large share of history to bring together the story for
this book, a record of the independence, commitment, and
courage of a remarkable black woman.

I would like to acknowledge the assistance of the other
people and institutional resources which have been indis-
pensable in the preparation of this book. Special mention
goes to Daniel T. Williams, Archivist of Tuskegee Institute.
I am indebted to Lucille A. Boykin of the Texas History and
Genealogy Division of the Dallas Public Library, Dorothea
L. Smart, Dean of Bradford College, and Mary Ann Ross of
Framingham State College, all of whom were most respon-
sive to my research needs. Acknowledgment is due to Pro-
fessor Louis R. Harlan, whose editing of *The Booker T.
Washington Papers* and scholarly biography of Washington
deserve the attention of all students of American history.
Grateful mention should be made of the Library of Con-
gress; the Moorland-Spingarn Research Center of Howard
University; and the vast research collections of The New
York Public Library (Astor, Lenox and Tilden Foundations), of which the Schomburg Center for Research in
Black Culture was invaluable.

Preface

A special thank you goes to James S. Haskins for his early assistance and encouragement and to Margo Jefferson, I also extend my thanks. As copy editor, Georgie Remer smoothed out the rough edges, to the gratitude of the author. Finally, I would like to thank Marie Brown, whose endurance and enthusiastic and perceptive editing, made it all worthwhile.

Ruth Ann Stewart

PORTIA

1

Like a Motherless Child

———————

Portia always knew that there was going to be something special about her life. She knew it almost from her birth, June 6, 1883, in the tiny rural town of Tuskegee, Alabama. She was born the first child and only daughter of Booker T. Washington and though the Washington name was as yet unknown, in his lifetime Booker was to become one of the most famous men recorded in American history. He founded one of the first schools of higher learning for black people in America, the Tuskegee Normal School for Colored Youth (now Tuskegee Institute), and built it into a base so powerful that it became known as the "Tuskegee Machine." He was to consort with Presidents and royalty and command the support of the wealthiest families of the nation. During the height of his career, he came to wield control over the destiny of black people to such an extent that few blacks moved up in the system without his knowledge and approval. Booker T. Washington stood as the power behind most of the black press and plotted the course of black economic development through his founding of the National Negro Business League. Although seeking no public office himself, he was to serve as the chief presidential adviser on Negro affairs including the determination of black (and southern white) political appointments.

A very complex man, Booker Taliaferro Washington was

1

both revered and hated to such an extent that even today, more than a half century after his death, his name still provokes a mixture of strong reactions. To the older generations, both black and white, he stands as a respected figure who did good things for his people and was a leader of his race. To the younger generations raised on urban riots, civil rights, and black power he was an Uncle Tom. Recent scholarship into the Washington myth has revealed that the truth about the man lies somewhere between these contradictory views, and to understand one must begin at the beginning.

Booker was born a slave in Franklin County, Virginia, less than a decade before the Civil War. He was told that the year of his birth was approximately 1856, but birth records were not kept for slaves so he could never be sure. His mother recalled it was in the spring, so Booker eventually selected April 5 as his birthday. His mother's name was Jane, but he knew nothing of his father except that he was a white man living, rumor had it, on a neighboring farm. Booker's gray eyes and light brown complexion clearly marked him as a white man's son, but the only father he was to know was later to be a stepfather, Washington Ferguson, from whom he took his last name. There is speculation that the name "Booker" might have been taken from a kindly master to whom Jane once belonged, but "Taliaferro" was an invention he believed of his mother's imagination.

Booker's household was completed by an older brother, John, and, later, a sister, named Amanda, fathered by Washington Ferguson. John was some three and a half years older than Booker and, though darker in complexion, also a mulatto. He was remembered as a quick, bright boy who willingly helped look after the younger children.

Booker was eight years old before he had his first pair of real shoes and older still before he sat down at a table for meals. Jane's duties as cook for their owners and the other slaves took most of her waking hours, leaving her family to fend for itself. Meals were leftover scraps from the master's table or what could be snatched on the run from the cooking fire. In even shorter supply was the mothering that growing children needed and craved. By nature, Jane was an affectionate woman but the heavy demands placed upon her by her kitchen duties and a history of poor health required that her children be self-sufficient from an early age. Hardly had Booker begun to walk when he was put to work fanning the flies from his master's dining table.

The family lived in a tiny cabin dominated by a large open fireplace constantly kept in use by Jane. Booker recalled that the warmth from the fireplace was welcomed in the winter time, but in summer it turned the cabin into an inferno. The cabin walls were constructed of loosely fitted boards lined with cracks that admitted the elements as freely as did the few glassless windows set into the walls. Furniture was nearly nonexistent, a pile of rags laid on the dirt floor serving as beds.

While their cabin was not untypical of the slave home, the traditional image of the antebellum southern plantation would have included a white-columned mansion with languishing aristocrats sipping mint juleps on a magnolia-shaded front porch. In actual fact, Booker's plantation was a two-hundred-seven-acre farm belonging to a dirt farmer named James Burroughs. The large Burroughs family was itself crowded together into a five-room house which sat with two slave cabins in a yard surrounded by a picket fence. Burroughs raised some tobacco for sale, but he was primarily a subsistence farmer who labored side by side with his slaves. The other slaves numbered about six, but Booker remembered little about them except one, Uncle Munroe, whom he saw stripped and beaten for some minor act of disobedience.

3

Even though many former slaveholders, including the Burroughses, were later to deny it, corporal punishment was a fact of slave life. The threat of punishment and death was an unifying reality that helped to hold the southern autocracy together. This sanction was especially effective in Booker's community because, unlike many areas in the South, blacks in Franklin County were in the minority. Booker was born a watcher, and in the slow, contemplative manner that was to become his hallmark, he came to respect at an early age what he saw as white power. His observations in the field and at the master's dining table provided the first cornerstones of his ultimate philosophy. The key to this power, it seemed to him, resided in the white man's knowledge of that larger world which was withheld by law from Booker and his race.

The laws imposed on slaves belie the image held by some that slave-master relations were family affairs nourished by benevolence and passivity. As the result of numerous slave insurrections, actual and feared, codes governing slave behavior had been enacted, beginning almost with the first arrival of abducted Africans in America in 1619 at Jamestown, Virginia. These Black Codes restricted the times and distances slaves could travel with a pass, and a lantern was required identification for any movement after dark. There were restrictions imposed on the numbers which could assemble in a group. In some cases, any more than two blacks together constituted a conspiracy. To teach a slave to read was forbidden.

Reading to blacks was permissible if confined to the Bible and even then, only to those passages interpreted as supporting the southern status quo. The closest young Booker came to reading was when, as a part of his duties, he accompanied his owner's daughter Laura to the local school where she taught. Before starting back with the horse for the day's

4

work, he would cautiously peep into the schoolhouse window. To be able to sit and study like the white children he observed, he recalled in his autobiography, *Up from Slavery*, seemed to him "about the same as getting into paradise." But his nirvana had to await the aftermath of that collision of social and economic factors which propelled the nation into a war from which it has yet to fully recover.

The Civil War, commenced in Booker's fifth or sixth year, he at first perceived only as something disquieting in the air of his backwoods community. As the conflict intensified, the war became more real, taking its toll of the white male population of Franklin County, including several members of the Burroughs family. Foodstuffs and materials became scarce, but only for whites, who were accustomed to a richer fare than the locally produced products upon which the slaves already had to survive. The real effect of the conflict on Booker's world was on the hopes which it stirred in the minds and hearts of his fellow slaves. Blacks sent on errands to town would lounge around afterward, appearing stereotypically lazy but with ears alert to discussion of the war among the whites. Each report of a Yankee advance went winging through the slave quarter and often in the traditional form of black expression, the spiritual. But now the singing was about release from care in this world and not having to wait for the next. The whispered conversations and furtive meetings about the prospect of freedom became more frequent until one morning Booker awoke to find his mother down on her knees openly praying over her children that the armies of the North be triumphant and set her people free.

When northern soldiers began to appear on the roads of Franklin County, they were greeted with increasing boldness by blacks bearing food and water. These were courageous acts for a powerless people who dwelled in a time and place nearly as hostile to men in blue uniforms as to men and women in black skins. But freedom was on its way and, just like the many runaway slaves who had joined the Union Army, the blacks of Franklin County were prepared to risk their lives to secure that freedom.

Emancipation, or Jubilee Day, as it was named by blacks, came to Franklin County soon after the close of the war in Booker's ninth year. The Burroughses' slaves were assembled before the main house, and as their former masters looked on, they were read the Emancipation Proclamation by a northern soldier. The words were particularly sweet to Jane as she joyfully hugged her young children, tears streaming down her face. She could not have envisioned the heights to which her middle child would rise, but with freedom she now had hope that her children would have a better life than the one she had known.

In the closing days of slavery, Jane had been allowed to marry Washington Ferguson, who lived on a neighboring farm. Though Ferguson had fathered Booker's sister, Amanda, being the property of a different master, he was required by southern law to live apart from his family. Wash, as he was known, was a restless man who refused to wear the shackles of slavery submissively. His owner found that the only way he could keep him in control was by contracting him to outside jobs. Wash was hired out to the railroad, to tobacco factories, and to the saltworks at Malden, in the new state of West Virginia. Sometime around 1864, after he had married Jane, while on one of these jobs he ran away with the Union Army. At the war's end, he settled in Malden and sent for his family. Jane immediately piled the family's few possessions into a horse-drawn wagon and with hardly a glance backward set out for her first home in freedom. The granite strength of this woman was never more clearly demonstrated than during this journey. Racked by asthma and generally worn out by her years of unrewarded labor, she nevertheless led her family over mountainous roads fraught with the dangers of a disintegrated social order. For two weeks she pushed her little band, bedding them down each night beside the road, with a sigh of relief that they had survived the day and with a prayer that the next would bring them closer to their journey's end.

The children enjoyed the trip as a great adventure, but Booker and his older brother John were to receive a rude awakening when they finally arrived in Malden. Hardly had they settled into the cabin secured by Wash for his family than they were put to work tending a furnace in the local saltworks. Under slavery both boys had learned the meaning of work, but their former drudgery was play compared to life in the saltworks. Wash was a hard worker, but wages were so paltry for freedmen that the few dollars more brought home by his young stepsons were necessary, he believed, for the basic survival of the family. Yet Wash was not an unkind man, adopting yet another child not of his flesh whom Jane found abandoned in a Malden barn and named James.

Booker hated his hot, dirty work at the furnaces, and even though devoted to his family, he came to resent his stepfather especially for taking all of his earnings. For Booker there had to be more meaning to freedom, and the key, it still seemed to him, lay in learning how to read. At some point in history, a story that Booker was taught to read by a white woman, perhaps even one of the Burroughs daughters, became part of the Washington myth. In actual fact it was through Booker's own effort that he mastered his first words. His mother was herself illiterate, but acutely sensitive to the awakening ambition in her second born. Somehow she secured for him one of the blue Webster word books popular in the schools of the day. With her encouragement and the tenacious determination that would make him famous, Booker taught himself the basic rudiments of reading while still working full time at the saltworks.

The first school Booker attended was started in 1865 in the section of Malden where most of the blacks lived, Tinkersville. It was held in the home of the Baptist minister, Lewis Rice, and also served as the African Zion Baptist Church on Wednesday evenings and Sundays. Father Rice, as he was affectionately known, had prevailed upon a literate black soldier from Ohio named William Davis to settle in Malden and establish the school. Davis and the school were entirely supported from the meager resources of the Tinkersville community, the town of Malden having chosen to ignore the state requirement that it provide a separate colored school where the number of eligible students exceeded thirty.

Once opened, the schoolhouse was filled day and night with people of all ages. As Booker was to recall in his autobiography, "It was a whole race trying to go to school. Few were too young, and none too old, to make the attempt to learn. As fast as any kind of teachers could be secured, not only were day schools filled, but night schools as well . . . Day schools, night schools, and Sunday schools were always crowded, and often many had to be turned away for want of room."

To Booker's great disappointment, he was only able to attend school at night. Wash refused to give up the earnings from his stepson's daytime labors, but, while having little regard for formal education himself, he did not stand in the way of Booker going to school on his own time. Once exposed to the classroom, Booker resolved that his job at the saltworks must end. His chance came when some time around the year of 1867 he became houseboy to the most prominent family in Malden, the Ruffners.

8

General Lewis Ruffner had been a slaveowner but he opposed Virginia's secession from the Union and, with the outbreak of the war, moved to help form the new state of West Virginia and served in the Union Army. While the general became a respected employer, it was to be his wife, Viola, who would have a profound effect upon the young black boy.

Viola Knapp Ruffner had been born one of seven children to Vermont parents of strong Yankee stock but limited resources. She educated herself and made her way through the only respectable profession open to women at the time, that of a teacher. She taught school in New England, New Jersey, and finally North Carolina from which she accepted the position as governess for the household headed by the widowed General Ruffner. Her eventual marriage to the general was greatly resented by his children. Highly intelligent and caring, Viola was deeply hurt by this rejection. Out of frustration, perhaps, she poured her vigorous energies into her home, making a reputation for herself as a hard taskmaster in the black community from which she drew her servants.

Booker entered a whole new world when he crossed the threshold of the Ruffner mansion. The contrast to what he had left behind must have stunned his young mind even though he was already in the process of moving away from his origins. The settlement of the Washington family in Malden had not been a pleasant experience for Booker. A country boy during his formative years, Booker's exposure to city life shocked him. Wash had chosen to live outside the black Tinkersville enclave, preferring rather an area which found blacks and poor whites living side by side in the same squalor. The noise produced by gambling and raucous late-night drinking parties by both groups in the garbage-laden streets of Booker's neighborhood grated on ears accustomed to the serenity of the countryside. The repugnance that Booker would always have for urban life had already begun to form, as well as the belief that poor whites were morally corrupt.

His move to the Ruffners' employment was a godsend but even at that, the transition was not an easy one. The price he had to pay for the refinement and luxury with which he was suddenly surrounded involved strict fidelity to every demand made by his new employer. Cleanliness, order, and honesty were the tenets by which his mistress ran her life. Every task to which he was assigned was judged by these criteria and where he was found lacking he was severely criticized. The work as a whole was light compared to the saltworks, but Booker learned to wash and clean with an intensity and diligence that forever afterward made him restless in slovenly surroundings.

He resisted total commitment to the Ruffners' way of life for a while by continuing to live at home and periodically seeking employment elsewhere, in coal mines and even once as a cabin boy assigned to a river boat which went as far as Cincinnati. But the lure of a genteel environment and the opportunity it provided, with Viola's tutoring and encouragement for continuation of his schooling, finally won him over. He came to live full time with Viola and the general, willingly embracing the white upper-class Yankee ethic that was in the process of forming yet another cornerstone of his philosophy toward life. A quiet but strong affection developed between the former schoolteacher and her young black houseboy. She recognized something special in him and was fulfilled in her own personal frustration by the intelligence, honesty, and industry with which he responded to her every demand.

While Booker flourished under this attention, making great strides in his ability to read and order his life, he never lost touch with the black community. He continued to turn over his wages to his family and was an active member of the Reverend Rice's church. But the dichotomy of his life began to make him restless. William Davis had turned out to be a gifted teacher whom Booker would always remember with fondness. But the black ex-soldier's education was limited and Booker became convinced that he had to seek outside of Malden for opportunities to advance himself. While working in a coal mine during one of his several departures from the Ruffners' employment, Booker overheard two miners discussing a school for advanced learning which had been started in Virginia for blacks. The school, the Hampton Normal and Agricultural Institute, allowed poor students to earn their tuition and board by doing manual labor. No stranger to work, Booker became determined to seek out this school. He was encouraged in his goal by William Davis' successor, Henry Clay Payne, who had come to Malden to teach after being graduated in one of the first classes at Hampton.

In 1872, at the age of sixteen, Booker finally set out on the long road to Hampton. Booker was aided by his mother and brother John especially and by contributions from the black community, which traditionally has pooled its meager resources to help one of theirs succeed to a better place in life. But even with this support, Booker's travel money soon ran out and he had to walk most of the five hundred miles to Hampton, Virginia. The journey took several months and included many cold night sleeps out of doors and hard work at odd jobs en route. He finally arrived at Hampton in October of 1872, ragged, penniless, and exhausted.

The first official he encountered was the person in charge of the women students, Hampton's Lady Principal, Mary F. Mackie. Miss Mackie, though born in Newburgh, New York, was cut from the same stern Yankee fabric that Booker had come to know and respect in Viola Ruffner. She was dismayed at Booker's appearance but through some second sight perceived his determination and allowed him bed and board for the night with a promise to review his qualifications after he rested. The next morning Booker's entrance exam was to be the cleaning of a classroom for the Lady Principal. Mustering all the experience he had gained from Viola Ruffner, Booker impressed Miss Mackie with an immaculate performance and thus commenced his Hampton days. He was to spend three years enrolled at Hampton, working the entire time as a janitor.

Hampton Normal and Agricultural Institute had been founded in 1868 as a vocational school for newly freed slaves. Little more than a secondary school, it was to eventually become a crucible for black talent in the new South. But in the beginning, the school emphasized the basics which its founders believed were most needed by the former slaves. Personal industry, hygiene, and racial uplift were the goals. Use of the toothbrush, proper nutrition, bodily cleanliness, the healthful benefits of fresh air and sunlight, manners, thriftiness, honesty, moral rectitude, and vocational training were the main areas of instruction.

In the time left over, there was instruction in the three R's but always oriented toward the practical training received, for example, in the school's dairy barn or the laundry. Mathematical problems were conceived in terms of cooking measures or brick-laying schemes. Reading about better ways of raising cattle or setting a table was the literature lesson. The staff was a dedicated group of white Northerners who came South after the Civil War to work with blacks, extending their services later to include Indians. Chief among these benefactors was General Samuel C. Armstrong, founder and head of Hampton. Though no less paternalistic than other liberals of his day (he was given to saying that life would not be worth living without the Negro and Indian problem), Armstrong had a strength of character and unselfish dedication that made him a truly remarkable man. He made a lasting impression on Booker, becoming his greatest friend and adviser.

Booker graduated Hampton with honors in 1875 and returned home to Malden to teach. He had been elected by the Tinkersville community to head the same school which three years earlier he himself had attended. His teaching certificate entitled him to a salary of $31.50 each month, now at least being paid by the county even though white male teachers received an average of $41.50 each month. Though his income was meager, the new teacher chose to set up his own household. Jane's frail health had finally given out the previous year, when she died quietly in her sleep. Booker perhaps wanted to avoid the additional strain on his sister, Amanda, who, at thirteen years of age, was struggling to keep house for her brother John and widowed father. But Booker was also a grown man of twenty and knew it was time to be on his own.

The school was open all hours of the day and night, crowded to the rafters with pupils ranging in age from seven to seventy. The older ones just wanted to learn to read the Bible before they died. The others knew their future depended on it. Special attention was given to the brightest students. Each year the three or four best were singled out and groomed for Hampton. It was perhaps among these special students that Booker first encountered Fanny Smith, the young woman who was to become his wife and the mother of his daughter, Portia.

Fanny Norton Smith was a striking woman whose white and Indian antecedents were evident in her light brown complexion, high cheekbones, and long, flowing black hair. She came to deeply love the stern and serious young teacher

13

despite the objections of her mother Celia Smith. Little is known of the Smith family or how it came to be in Malden, but Celia had high expectations for her beautiful daughter and looked upon Booker as a poor prospect.

Much to Celia's relief, their courtship was curtailed when in 1878 Booker went to Washington, D.C., for a year of study at a small black Baptist theological school named Wayland Seminary.

The exact reasons for this departure are lost in history but it appears that the young teacher underwent a severe reassessment of his career goals. He had a mild interest in law while still in Malden but was subsequently drawn toward the Baptist Church, in which he was active as both a deacon and a Sunday school teacher. He observed the strong moral influence that his Malden minister, Lewis Rice, exerted over the local black community and thought, perhaps, that he could serve both his own ambitions and his people by becoming a Baptist preacher. Traditionally, from Northerner Adam Clayton Powell, Jr., to Southerner Martin Luther King, Jr., the preacher has been one of the most unifying and powerful forces in the black community. Besides, Fanny Smith's family could no longer object to a suitor pursuing so esteemed a profession.

The Reconstruction period had run its course by the time Booker arrived in Washington. During that period of federal control of the South, blacks had enjoyed some measure of the economic and political security promised to them by the Emancipation Proclamation. The District of Columbia had been the fountainhead of that power and blacks had gathered within its boundaries in large numbers. By 1900 there would be over eighty thousand black residents in the District. In 1878 Booker encountered a vigorous black community possessed of a sophistication and concern for materialist goals beyond his country-boy grasp. He was appalled by what he saw as the assumption of middle-class trappings, such as fine clothes and liberal arts education, which were so counter to his southern experience and Hampton training. The Wayland students were provided with their education without resort to self-help or training in practical skills, a system that would henceforth make higher education anathema to Booker. Just as in childhood, urban life repelled him and he was not sorry to put Washington behind him when he received in the spring of 1879 a letter from Armstrong requesting his return to Hampton. His assignment was as housemaster and teacher to the first group of American Indians enrolled at Hampton. By this time Fanny had entered the Institute so Booker was even more eager to return to his alma mater.

Booker's happy association with Hampton came to an end when, in May of 1881, General Armstrong received a letter from Tuskegee, Alabama, requesting that he recommend a candidate for principal of a Negro normal school to be established in the town. The search committee of prominent Tuskegee citizens approved of Hampton's philosophy of vocational training and was seeking someone from the school's staff or any other white man Armstrong recommended. The general responded that "The only man I can suggest is one Mr. Booker Washington a graduate of this institution, a very competent capable mulatto, clear headed, modest, sensible, polite and a thorough teacher and superior man. The best man we ever had here." Even though they had in mind a white man, they accepted the general's recommendation within a week, and by June 24, 1881, Booker had arrived in Tuskegee to begin his life's work.

He started the Tuskegee Normal School for Colored Youth on a $2,000-appropriation from the state of Alabama. This grant had been the result of a political deal. The Democratic candidate in the state senate race of 1880, Colonel Wilbur

F. Foster, promised a normal school to the Tuskegee black community in exchange for its vote. The idea had been that of a black resident of the town, Lewis Adams, himself semiliterate and a moderately successful tinsmith, who believed that education was the key to real freedom.

The school opened July 4 in the African Methodist Episcopal Church with an enrollment of some thirty students ranging in age from sixteen to forty. The school soon moved to a dilapidated farm south of the town which Booker had borrowed $500 to purchase. From the start, Booker was convinced that the school had to be self-sufficient in both funding and operation. Dependence on state funds in a time and place generally hostile to black education of any kind could only lead to an uncertain future. Thus the farm land from the beginning was deeded by Booker to a board of trustees.

Steeped in the Hampton tradition, Booker founded the school as a vocational training school. The dignity of manual labor was fundamental to the philosophy on which Booker was to build his entire career. It seemed clear to him that blacks had to acquire skills whereby they could get jobs, buy property, and take care of their families. These skills had to be socially acceptable to whites as well as economically viable. The white man had been closely studied by the shrewd ex-slave. He understood their fears—even the most liberal secretly had them—that book-educated blacks would seek social equality (read "interracial sex" and "marriage between white women and black men"). It seemed to Booker that such a prospect was a long way off for the masses of black people and would work its own self out after blacks had gained economic equity for themselves.

That the struggle was to be a long one was borne in on Booker his first days in Alabama. Rural blacks were still living much in the way they had lived under slavery, with abysmal housing, nutrition, health care, and farming methods. He designed the Tuskegee experiment to be a total experience for the men and women who entered. From the time they rose in the early morning until they fell exhausted into bed at night, every aspect of their lives was structured and supervised by their determined principal. The lessons of the toothbrush and personal hygiene learned at Hampton were passed on to this new generation of students. Punctuality, honesty, and orderliness were constantly hammered home in class and by example. The virtues of work and pride in a job well done were emphasized as being almost rewards sufficient unto themselves.

Starting literally from scratch, the students plank by plank and later brick by brick built the school, often with their principal laboring by their side. Booker was a hard taskmaster but the students responded with enthusiasm. They too became caught up in the vision he had for the black race.

Booker's attention was not wholly consumed by work. He had kept up his courtship of Fanny Smith and upon her graduation from Hampton he returned home to claim her as his bride. They were married August 2, 1882, by Father Rice in the little Baptist Church in Malden. Portia described her mother as having had many admirers among her fellow students, some of whom were quite dashing and full of fun. "It came as a shock," Portia remembered being told, "when she finally chose the gawky country boy who only seemed interested in work and education, but Booker was a proper southern gentleman and waited until Fanny finished her education before carrying her off."

Fanny was a quiet, beautiful woman whose arrival at Tuskegee substantiated Booker's commitment to the school. They moved into a large house near the campus which they shared with the teaching staff, now grown to four. Never more than an average student, Fanny assumed the role of housekeeper, leaving the teaching functions to the single members of the household. But Fanny shared her husband's vision and frequently took the lead in seeking funds for the school. The person she seemed to turn to most often was Booker's old mentor General Armstrong. The general was drawn to her mother, Portia felt, because of his concern for Indians, whose blood also ran in Fanny's veins.

Out of this happy union of the sober ex-slave and the graceful Fanny was born, June 6, 1883, a daughter, Portia Marshall Washington. She was named Portia for the heroine of Shakespeare's *Merchant of Venice,* a favorite play of her father's. Her middle name was that of Hampton's treasurer, James Fowle Baldwin Marshall. Marshall had been Booker's strongest support at Hampton in the beginning days of Tuskegee. General Armstrong was in Europe for the summer and it had been left to Marshall to secure teaching materials for the first Tuskegee students. Perhaps out of sentimental gratitude or more pragmatically out of the recognition that Marshall controlled Hampton's purse strings, Portia was so named. The name Armstrong, Booker's great friend and mentor, was perhaps being reserved for the male children Booker hoped to father.

But tragically, his life with his first love was to be brief. Fanny was returning from a fund-raising picnic for Tuskegee when she fell out of a wagon. She never recovered from the injuries she incurred and spent her last days confined to a wheel chair, dying in the spring of 1884. Booker was described to Portia as "nearly going wild" when her mother died. But Booker was a man of carefully controlled emotions, whose public mourning could be confined to a tightly worded statement in his autobiography: "From the first, my wife most earnestly devoted her thoughts and time to the work of the school, and was completely one with me in every interest and ambition."

Bereft of his helpmate and mother for his child, Booker turned to Fanny's family for comfort. Portia's grandmother, Celia Smith, came to care for her for a brief time. She was affectionate and tenderhearted, but the Alabama climate did not agree with her, so she had to leave her granddaughter to the care of strangers. Booker took as active a role in his infant daughter's life as he could, but much of his time was spent on the road publicizing Tuskegee and raising funds for its operation.

He was aided in his travels by a brilliant and beautiful Hampton Institute graduate, Olivia Davidson, whom he had appointed assistant principal of Tuskegee. Olivia had been graduated from Hampton in 1879 and had gone on to complete a degree in education at Framingham State Normal School (now Framingham State College) in Massachusetts. Her tuition was paid by a wealthy Hampton donor, and she graduated two years later with distinction. During her time at Framingham, she came in contact with many white New Englanders of wealth and influence who were impressed with her intelligence and maturity. It was to these contacts that she now turned for assistance for Tuskegee. With her guidance, Booker began to travel a northern fund-raising circuit that would spell the success of Tuskegee but would increasingly absent him from home.

At first Portia mourned her father's departures, but he would send her picture postcards and surprise her with little gifts upon his return. Though weary from his travels, he would nestle Portia in his lap and tell her stories, especially the fairy tales of the brothers Grimm. Portia prized these intimate moments, and even though her father presented a stern face to the world, she remembered him as a kind, affectionate man who imparted to her a secure sense of being loved. On only one issue did they seem to have a major disagreement. Booker was a dollar-and-cents man, who believed in the power of money to a people only a few years out of slavery. As Portia grew older, he insisted that she learn mathematics well. She hated the subject and remembered her father's stern admonition to "Get that math, Portia."

But she was his firstborn and he could never be hard with her for long. Her actual care was taken over by women members of the Tuskegee staff who would board at the principal's home. This exposure to a variety of attendant personalities at so young an age probably helped to shape Portia's independent, outgoing nature. But her father was not a man who could tolerate such instability for his child nor loneliness for himself long. In 1885 he took a second wife, his assistant principal, Olivia A. Davidson.

Olivia had been born June 11, 1854, in Tazewell County, Virginia. With the ending of slavery, her family migrated to Albany, Ohio, where she was educated at a private black school, the Albany Enterprise Academy. She taught for a while in Memphis, Tennessee, before entering Hampton Institute. Her academic background had been so good that she was graduated after only one year of study before going on for further study at Framingham.

At Tuskegee, Olivia taught science, literature, and bookkeeping. But her main, almost missionarylike concern was making the female students over into copies of the gently bred ladies she had encountered in New England. From Olivia, Portia received her share of training in deportment and willingly so because she grew to love Olivia, calling her "Mama." Portia's stepmother brought order and grace into the Washington household. She smoothed off the rough edges of Booker's country manner and coached him into the oratorical brilliance that was to help make him famous. Out of this fortuitous union there were born two sons, Booker T. Washington II and Ernest Davidson Washington.

Portia's first brother, Booker II, was born in Boston during the summer of 1886. The Washingtons were in Massachusetts because of a health and physical fitness course Booker was attending at Harvard. Olivia's instincts proved correct and increasingly Booker had extended his successful fund-raising efforts into the North, concentrating on the New England states. He was on the road much of the school year now and the hectic pace he maintained had brought him to the point of collapse. After seeing him so fatigued, Olivia had arranged this respite at Harvard, even to obtaining the money to pay his expenses from one of her Yankee contacts.

Three years later, their second son, Ernest, was born at Tuskegee. In spite of her seemingly endless vitality and drive, Olivia had never been a strong woman. She had suffered several collapses in her lifetime, one of which had nearly prevented her from first coming to Tuskegee. The birth of her second child appeared to sap her final reserve of energy. When Booker saw that she was not regaining her strength, he moved her to the Massachusetts General Hospital in Boston, where three months later, on May 9, 1889, she died.

Booker was a crushed man. He had stayed in attendance at her hospital bedside the whole time, watching with fear and anguish her gradual demise. For the second time, he had lost the woman he loved and an invaluable helpmate in the cause he loved. Booker returned to Tuskegee, faced again with the full responsibility of child raising, but now there were three to care for. Though mature for her age, Portia was still a child. Booker perhaps reflected on his sister's unsuccessful attempt to keep the family together after their mother's death. Portia and her brothers had to have a better life. But the fund raising demands of Tuskegee made it impossible for him to be the full-time parent that his family required.

21

A temporary solution was found when his brother, John, took over the Washington brood. John and his wife provided a stability that sustained the children during their father's frequent absences. Being older, Portia could be made to understand why Papa, as she called him, had to be away so much. She came to accept his departures without tears, promising him to save up all the news for his return. When she could prevail upon someone to write a letter for her, she would dictate very chatty and gay messages, ending with, "come home soon to your loving, little Portia." Portia adored her father and in her child's mind perhaps began to see herself as something more than just a daughter. She was very motherly toward her brothers, remembering perhaps how much she had missed not having a mother herself. She felt that the only person she could talk to was her father and would usually keep her thoughts to herself until he came home.

In the summer of 1890 Booker hired a nursemaid, Mrs. Dora S. King, who took Portia, then seven years of age, and her brothers home with her to Hanover, Massachusetts, for a visit. A strong indication that Portia had begun to assign to herself heavier responsibilities than a child her age should have shouldered is revealed in a letter Dora wrote to Booker.

Hanover, Mass. Sept. 5/90

Mr. Washington:

. . . The children are all well, and Portia begins to show the benefit of her summer's visit. She put on a dress the other day that she had not worn for four or five weeks, and she laughed to find that it had grown both tight and short. She shows as great a change in temperament as in physique, she is so much more cheerful and childlike than she was. She sleeps well and as a child should and has an excellent appetite . . .

D. S. King

Booker's concern for his motherless children was probably a strong influence in his decision to marry a third and, as it proved, final time. As once before, he made his selection from within the Tuskegee community. He chose a teacher of English, Margaret James Murray. Margaret had been born into a large family of slaves in Macon, Mississippi, at the close of the Civil War. From age seven she lived with a Quaker family who took special interest in her education. She attended Fisk University, in Nashville, Tennessee, where on her graduation day in June 1889 she met Booker T. Washington. Maggie, as Booker was to call her, was seated opposite Booker at the graduation luncheon, and "without knowing just how it came about," she was later to say, she found herself on her way to Tuskegee.

Maggie was a vigorous, intelligent woman whose wide interests and refinement made her an excellent complement to Tuskegee's principal. Their relationship was slow in evolving into anything less than professional, but by the summer of 1892 Booker had prevailed upon Maggie to consent to become his wife. While Maggie had deep feelings for Booker, she had resisted the prospects of marrying him because of his family. She knew nothing of children and child rearing and Booker had an active brood of three. The boys were young enough to give over to the care of nursemaids, but Portia was nearly ten and grown to an independence beyond her years. She was clearly the apple of her father's eye and looked with jealousy upon anyone who would be a rival for his affection. Portia wanted a mother and knew she and the boys needed a mother, but Maggie was cool and distant and could not fulfill Portia's desire for warmth and affection.

Maggie was keenly aware of this antagonism and wrote to Booker, "You have no idea how I feel because I can not feel toward Portia as I should. And I somehow dread being thrown with her for a life time." Characteristically, Booker tried to mediate the tense relationships between the two females in his life. He could not dismiss the feelings of his beloved daughter and yet he needed the companionship of a strong woman like Maggie.

Booker's will was to prevail and he and Maggie were unceremoniously married at Tuskegee in October 1893. In spite of her obstinacy, Portia was a dutiful daughter and promised to try to get along with her new stepmother. Their contact was to be minimized because of the traveling Maggie did with her husband on many of his fund-raising trips for the Institute. She was also involved with a professional life of her own as Tuskegee's Lady Principal and as president of the Southern Federation of Colored Women's Clubs, whose magazine she edited as well. Part of Maggie's problem was solved when Portia enrolled, along with her oldest brother, in the Tuskegee training school.

The truce was not an easy one as poignantly revealed in a letter she wrote to her father November 19, 1893:

> Pappa, I try to make people love me but one habit I try and outgrow is being slow. It is pretty hard because the hardest . . . [scolding] I ever got from mama [was] because I did not get the children's room cleaned up fast enough that night. I said I'm not going to try to please mama she's to hard to suit but a book I read gave me better thoughts. Sometimes [I] feel as if I have no friends in the world and I just cry and mama will say, "Portia what are you crying about?" But I never tell her. I all ways tell you my thoughts because I think you will like to hear them.

During her father's absence Portia's chief source of comfort became music. At an early age she had displayed an interest in music, reaching up to finger the keys of an old organ in the house. When she could reach the keyboard, Booker installed a piano and arranged for one of the Institute's staff members to give her lessons. She started with simple keyboard exercises and nursery rhymes, perfected under the guidance of her teacher in the evenings after school. Much to her father's delight, she took to the piano with the same kind of intensity he gave to the affairs of the Institute. Her progress was rapid, and by the age of ten she had memorized a number of Negro spirituals and could sight-read several of the simpler classics. His daughter's time and energies were being used constructively and, to both his and Maggie's relief, Portia seemed content. Booker could now travel with more peace of mind.

Portia's love of music was unprecedented in the Washington family. Neither Booker nor Portia's mother or stepmothers had displayed a particular interest in music. Church-centered music was an integral part of black life, and from his earliest days at Tuskegee Booker had included spirituals in the school's evening and Sunday prayer services. It was natural that the first full compositions Portia mastered would be spirituals. Negro spirituals had by this time been annotated and published to wide acclaim, especially after the success of the Fisk Jubilee Singers. This chorus of some dozen young black men and women students had gone out from Fisk University in 1866 to raise money on a triumphal tour of the northeastern United States and Europe.

At Tuskegee, Portia grew up on this same music, bringing to the sheet music she beheld before her the additional dimension of emotion. She perceived in the voices of the ex-slaves and the sons and daughters of slaves who lifted their voices in the Tuskegee chapel the source of these mostly sorrowful songs. She embraced this sorrow through her music and melded it with her own, playing most often the song "Sometimes I Feel Like a Motherless Child."

Booker loved to hear his daughter practicing, and as much for him as for herself she disciplined herself to spend long hours at the piano. When home, Portia remembered that her father would listen from his study, keeping the door open while he worked on his voluminous correspondence or his latest speech. Booker had become much sought-after as a spokesman for black people, and with each speaking engagement his skill and reputation as a persuasive orator had grown. By the last decade of the nineteenth century, the gains made by southern blacks during Reconstruction had all but disappeared. "Jim Crow" reigned unchallenged, especially in the area of education. Funds for black schools had dried up to a trickle. But Tuskegee was flourishing and that was because the Washington brand of education had found favor with whites both North and South.

Tuskegee was a training school that emphasized hard, physical labor as a virtue unto itself. Looking on from the outside, the white world could only approve of Booker's methods. He appeared to be successfully teaching the best of American virtues in a manner that would keep black people quiet and contained. Skills were being acquired that could serve the South while maintaining the Negro in his traditional role as a beast of burden. Booker dismissed the growing number of critics who pointed the racist implications of this policy out to him. He believed that he knew what was best for the rural South and was confirmed in his belief by the generous response of white philanthropy and the successes that still lay ahead.

The event that catapulted Booker into national fame and conferred on him the title of "race leader" took place in Portia's twelfth year. Portia said she always felt her father was someone out of the ordinary but she never really knew how much so until September 18, 1895, when Booker had been invited to address the Cotton States Exposition at Atlanta, Georgia.

Portia was seated early in the gallery just opposite the stage of the great Exposition Hall with her stepmother and two brothers. As the hall slowly filled, she recalled, her excitement grew: "Oh how the colored people came and all those important white people, all there to see my father!" Tense with anticipation, she watched her father mount the stage and stand quietly behind the lectern until the vast audience began to settle down and fix its attention on the lone man of color standing calmly before them.

A contemporary account by a New York newspaper conveys the mood and significance of that occasion:

> There was a remarkable figure, tall, bony, straight as a Sioux chief, high forehead, straight nose, heavy jaws, and strong determined mouth, with big white teeth, piercing eyes, and commanding manner. The sinews stood out on his bronze neck and his muscular right brown fist. His big feet were planted squarely, with the heels together and the toes turned out. His voice rang out clear and true, and he paused impressively as he made each point.
>
> Within ten minutes the multitude was in an uproar of enthusiasm—handkerchiefs were waved, canes were flourished, hats were tossed in the air. The fairest women of Georgia stood up and cheered . . .
>
> I have heard the great orators of many countries, but not even Gladstone himself could have pleaded a cause with more consummate power than this angular Negro standing in a nimbus of sunshine surrounded by the men who once fought to keep his race in bondage. The roar might swell ever so high, but the expression of his earnest face never changed.

Portia was swept with overwhelming pride as the audience leaped to its feet in unanimous approval of her father. She did not understand at that time the full implication of the speech which first articulated the controversial Washington propoundings: "In all things that are purely social we can be as separate as the fingers, yet one as the hand in all things essential to mutual progress . . . Cast down your bucket where you are . . . Cast it down in agriculture, mechanics, in commerce, in domestic service, and in the professions . . . We shall prosper in proportion as we learn to dignify and glorify common labor and put brains and skills into the common occupation of life."

In the simplest of language, Booker T. Washington had laid out a blueprint for black social and economic development which would be embraced by white America as *the* solution to the Negro problem. With this one statement, Tuskegee was to become the standard by which black achievement was judged and its founder and principal the arbitrator of the relationship between the races in the United States. There were, however, some people both black and white who would view the Washington ascendancy with alarm. Almost immediately, this small but vocal group would come out in opposition to the Washington doctrine as condemning the black race to menial labor and second-class citizenship. Unknown to Portia, the lines were drawn that day for a battle which would affect the rest of her life.

But for the moment, Portia felt only exhilaration and believed that her father had saved the day for the colored race. She remembered seeing "a mob of rednecks formed up beside the stage waiting to set upon my Pa if he had said but one word against the South." By the time he had finished speaking, they were wildly applauding and slapping their thighs in approval of what the black man had said.

Suddenly Booker was a national celebrity. He was invited to be a judge of the awards for the Exposition and received official congratulations and a visit from President Grover Cleveland. Many, many years later, Portia remarked, "just think, I was the daughter of a man who received the President of the United States."

Heady with the success of her father's speech and all that she had experienced in the city of Atlanta, Portia returned to Tuskegee. It was to be a brief homecoming because Portia's destiny had begun to take recognizable shape. Her sheltered southern days were at an end and the specialness she had always felt was about to begin. Arrangements had been made for her that fall of 1895 to enter her first stepmother Olivia Davidson Washington's former school, Framingham State Normal School.

A little frightened, still not knowing completely what it was all about, Portia kissed Maggie and her brothers good-by, and with the final encouraging words of her father, she boarded a train headed north to Massachusetts.

2

You Can't Go Home Again

The Alabama countryside rushed by as the Southern Railway train gained speed, quickly leaving behind all that was most familiar to Portia. She pressed her face against the window, straining for a final glimpse of childhood landmarks. But Portia was never to be a person who looked back long. Smoothing her bodice, she arranged her skirt like the lady she remembered Olivia Davidson had instructed her to be and settled down in her seat to face what lay ahead.

Seated opposite her was Robert W. Taylor, the first of many chaperones that were to be imposed upon Portia by her father. Taylor was one of several agents employed by Tuskegee to raise funds in the North. He was a dignified black man whose vested suit and starched white collar gave him an air of distinction. Booker was an admired employer and Taylor treated Portia with great ceremony. He had turned his seat backward, allowing Portia the full seat opposite while also being able to keep her completely in view.

Coming to collect their tickets, the conductor took exception to this black man riding backward and taking up so much room. When Taylor ignored his complaint, the conductor became enraged and attacked him, tearing his vest and cutting his lip with the ticket puncher. Taylor moved to defend himself, finally restraining the trainman with the aid of the other passengers. Portia was shaken by the incident. She had never been exposed to the violence of racial conflict. But she was calmed by the manner in which Taylor quickly regained his composure and settled down for the rest of the trip as if nothing had happened. Portia learned later that the conductor was fired after a simple word from her father to William H. Baldwin, Jr., who just happened to be the vice president of the Southern Railroad and a member of the Tuskegee board of trustees. Again Portia marveled at the power within her father's grasp.

At Framingham, Portia was quickly placed under the watchful eye of people who had been friends of her first stepmother. The memory of Olivia and the close ties cultivated by Booker and Maggie on their many trips north prepared the way for a warm reception. Chief among Portia's benefactors were Mary C. Moore, an English teacher, and the school's principal, Ellen Hyde, whose cousin Elizabeth Hyde taught at Hampton Institute. Portia was to be enrolled in the Practice School which Miss Hyde had been proudly developing for over a decade. Miss Moore was to look after Portia in a more personal way, she having been the person most instrumental in bringing Portia to Framingham after hearing of Booker's unsuccessful attempts to enroll his daughter in other northern schools.

Miss Moore had eagerly agreed to act *in loco parentis* but Portia was actually to board in Normal Hall, a dormitory. She had a pleasant little room that looked out on a campus of stately trees and ivy-covered buildings. Tuskegee Institute was a fledgling compared to Framingham, which had been founded in 1839 as the first state-supported normal school in the United States. It was steeped in tradition which Portia came to regard deeply. But she refused to be awed by her surroundings. After all, she was Booker T. Washington's daughter, with a special heritage of her own.

Her pride was sometimes to get her into trouble, but it also sustained her through many lonely days. Her fellow residents in Normal Hall were older students enrolled in the normal school. The contact with them probably further accelerated her maturity but left her in want of companionship. She was cut off from her peers much of the time because the Practice School students commuted each day from the surrounding towns. Years later Grace F. Shepard, an English instructor, was to recall her impressions of Portia at the time:

> . . . Her life was unnatural and rather sad I used to think. She had no companions of her own age except for the occasional visits of Miss Moore's niece Mary Shattuck. Then the little blonde and the little negro [*sic*] would play together in the grove with Miss Moore's tricycle.

Perhaps the years had dimmed and mellowed Portia's memory of her early school days. Looking back, she felt only fondness for Framingham. It was there that she was first exposed to high-level music training. Her piano teacher had been educated at the New England Conservatory of Music and conducted a small studio in the center of town. Several times each week, Portia would board the horse-drawn Framingham Union Railroad and journey to her piano lessons. The lonely hours were filled with preparation for these encounters and she recalled the excitement she felt at her growing skillfulness.

When it became known that "the little negro" could really handle herself at the piano, some of Portia's loneliness was abated. She was called upon to play for all the dances held at the school. The same Grace Shepard recalled:

> She was a very lively little girl, fond of music and brilliant in playing for dances. She would sit on the

piano stool as though constructed of wire springs and operated by electric power—head turned back over her shoulder to watch the dancers, and fingers moving as of their own volition. She wanted to dance, poor child, but the students of the Normal School were never ready to release her. No one could play like Portia, and Portia uncomplainingly and very generously constantly contributed to our social happiness in this way.

Even though it may have appeared that Portia wanted to dance, if asked she would most likely have refused. As Booker T. Washington's daughter, she understood and accepted the invisible line that in all things social separated her from her white peers. She envisioned herself as a special guest in the white world she now inhabited and seized any and all opportunities which confirmed her uniqueness. She embraced her role as entertainer with enthusiasm, enjoying immeasurably her few moments in the spotlight.

Music was to change another dimension of Portia's life while at Framingham. One Sunday she was taken by Miss Moore to the local Protestant Episcopal church. Portia was fascinated by the ritual and liturgical music so different from the Baptist services on which she had been raised. She returned Sunday after Sunday and eventually undertook the formal instruction necessary to be confirmed an Episcopalian.

Her decision to convert was made only after consultation with her father. Even though Booker seemed always to be on the move, he kept in constant touch with Portia through short, pithy letters. His travels frequently brought him to Boston where, whenever possible, he would board the horse-car for Framingham.

As in most things that he did as principal of Tuskegee, Booker combined these visits with official Institute business. Taking a cue from the success of the Fisk Jubilee Singers,

Above left,
Booker T. Washington at the time he
founded Tuskegee Institute, 1881.
*Schomburg Center, The New York
Public Library, Astor, Lenox and
Tilden Foundations*

Above right,
Portia's mother, Fanny Smith
Washington, c. 1882. *Tuskegee
Institute Archives*

Bottom,
Portia's first stepmother,
Olivia Davidson Washington, c. 1887.
*The New York Public Library,
Astor, Lenox and Tilden Foundations*

Above, The Washington Family, 1895:
Ernest Davidson; Booker, Jr.;
Margaret Murray Washington;
Booker T. Washington; Portia.
Tuskegee Institute Archives

Right, Portia during the time she
was enrolled at Framingham State
Normal School, c. 1897, the first of
several exclusive New England
schools she attended. *The New York
Public Library, Astor, Lenox and
Tilden Foundations*

Left, Mary C. Moore, teacher of
English and the person most
responsible for Portia attending the
New England school.
Framingham State College

Below, Normal Hall, Portia's dormitory
while attending the practice school at
Framingham State Normal School.
Framingham State College

Left, The eminent black scholar W. E. B. Du Bois, c. 1896, soon after his return from the University of Berlin and before his schism with Booker T. Washington.
Schomburg Center, The New York Public Library, Astor, Lenox and Tilden Foundations

Below, The Oaks, official Tuskegee residence of the Washington family. *Library of Congress*

Booker would frequently travel in the North with student singers from Tuskegee. His visits to Framingham with this group were recalled some years later by Grace Shepard, writing from Wheaton College in Norton, Massachusetts, for an "historical sketch" of Framingham published in 1914:

> When Booker T. Washington was a younger man, he used to visit Framingham to cheer the students with accounts of progress at Tuskegee. He used to bring the quartette and stay a day or two to inspect our school and gather inspiration for his own work. The faculty on such occasions took dinner together in Crocker Hall with these earnest, gifted young men for guests, and the girls gathered on the stairway in the early evening to hear Old Black Joe, Swing Low Sweet Chariot, and other negro melodies sung as only negroes can sing them, song after song from willing artists who grudged no encores.

Tuskegee was well known to the Framingham community where it had become a tradition over the years to contribute clothes and money to the black school. Just that spring, prior to Portia's enrollment, an Easter chapel offering had been collected especially for Tuskegee. Booker, with first Olivia and then Maggie, mined the missionary inclinations of these more affluent New Englanders for his fledgling institution. Where money was not forthcoming, he accepted used clothes which were refitted in the Tuskegee sewing classes for students who in most cases possessed little beyond their desire for an education.

Portia encouraged these contributions from Framingham, knowing full well the needs of Tuskegee. But she could not stand being looked upon as a charity case by association. She strove to distinguish herself in her studies and music but was especially strengthened when Booker visited the school. Her adoration for him had only increased with her absence from home. Proudly she would accompany him around the campus, aglow with happiness at his presence and the status it afforded her. She reveled in the dignity of his carriage and the respect accorded to him by the faculty and administrators. Her peers took notice and once again she could find happiness in the spotlight she so craved.

On one occasion while at Framingham, her need for identification with her father proved to be somewhat of a public embarrassment. As Portia remembered it, "I went to a meeting my father had at a big theater in Boston . . . I went in to town with a teacher, a Canadian woman, and she loved Booker Washington—right after he made his Atlanta speech. Oh, the place was packed. His guests were Dr. Du Bois and the poet [Paul Laurence] Dunbar. Dunbar and his wife were both our friends. And they were all there on the platform . . . I rushed down the aisle and climbed up in my Papa's lap and hugged him and kissed him right before everybody. I was oblivious—just saw my daddy. And my father looked so glad to see me and all. Oh, the colored people thought it was terrible. My stepmother thought it was wrong of me to go up there and get in his lap. But I did what I wanted to do!"

When school closed for the summer, Portia returned to Tuskegee. She had caught a glimpse of a larger world and home now meant only hot, dusty Alabama days and the restraints of living with her stepmother, Maggie. Her longing to be away were expressively evident in a letter she wrote to Booker from Washington, D.C., during a short trip there with Maggie.

July 24, 1896

My dear papa—

. . . Yesterday we went to a charming little place on the Chesapeake Bay. I went in bathing nearly all morn-

ing and would have gone in the afternoon also if
mamma had been willing . . .

I am simply in love with Washington. I wish I could
see more of it. I hope someday when you come here to
stay any length of time you will bring me with you . . .

With much love, I am,

Your loving daughter

Portia

Booker was not insensitive to his daughter's unhappiness.
By the end of the summer she had been sent to vacation in
Hopedale, Massachusetts. Thereafter, Hopedale was to be
her home each summer while attending Framingham. Portia's hostess was the sister of Mary Moore, her Framingham
mentor. But she often saw her family because they came to
stay not too far away. The Washingtons frequently occupied
a house located near Boston, in Weymouth, Massachusetts,
that had been given to them rent free by the railroad man
William Baldwin.

Baldwin was a trustee of Tuskegee Institute and through
the years had become Booker's closest white friend and adviser. General Armstrong, Booker's Hampton mentor, had
died in 1893, leaving a void in the black man's life that was
filled by this Harvard-trained, northern aristocrat. Baldwin
brought the same business acumen which he exercised as
vice president of the Southern Railroad to the affairs of the
Institute and helped put it on a sound, working basis. Until
his death in 1905, his stature and personal generosity to the
Washington family made Boston the base for Booker's
northern activities.

With busy summers and even busier school terms, the
years at Framingham passed quickly. Before Portia knew
it, her graduation from grammar school had arrived and she
was faced—in 1899—with the sobering prospect of having to

return to Tuskegee. That she must come home had been gradually spelled out to her in her father's letters.

Booker had come under increasing criticism for maintaining his daughter in a northern white school. Questions were being raised about his credibility as the chief espouser of social separatism and vocational training in view of his own child's position. In retrospect, to know Booker T. Washington is to understand this duality. From his first exposure to Lewis and Viola Ruffner back in Malden when he was a boy, he had striven to align himself philosophically and in private life style with upper-class whites. He had gone on to discover firsthand through Olivia the cultural and social benefits of New England white education. From an early age his daughter had demonstrated an intelligence and musical precociousness that would be better nourished in an environment other than that provided by a training school. But Booker would brook no chinks in the powerful base that he had built, even for his beloved daughter, so Portia was summoned home. She was sixteen and on the brink of adulthood. But it was 1899 and the Victorian age closely regulated the behavior of single females. She had no alternatives. Because she trusted in her father and was a dutiful daughter, she acceded to his wishes.

Portia came home and enrolled at Tuskegee as a student of dressmaking. She felt like a sea gull, netted, and brought to roost in a chicken house. Gone were the freedom of dormitory living and the gay evenings of musical entertainments. Life in The Oaks, the name given to the principal's house, meant household chores performed under the watchful eye of her stepmother. As the daughter of the revered principal, her deportment had to be above reproach. Publicly Booker would permit no special favors for his daughter. The pampering that had been so much a part of her life at Framingham was a thing of the past. But the most

unbearable part of her homecoming was dressmaking. There
is little wonder that she hated it when one reads the description Maggie wrote for the book *Tuskegee and Its People*,
under the heading "What Girls Are Taught":

> The large class of the Dressmaking Division [spends]
> . . . the day from seven until half past five making the
> blue uniform dresses, filling orders for tailor-made
> dresses in silk and cloth, measuring, drafting, cutting,
> and fitting . . .

But Portia persevered, deflating her father's critics and
enabling him "to save face." She even enrolled, at Booker's
request, in a chemistry course taught by Dr. George Washington Carver. She disliked chemistry because of the math,
her old nemesis, but was grateful later for the contact it afforded her with that great scientist. It was always to be Portia's way to make the best of a situation. Her spirit and
spunk remained undaunted, and she even reached a rap-
proachement with Maggie that brought peace into The
Oaks.

The peace was a fragile one and remained intact only
because of the release Portia found in her music. She practiced the Brahms and Bach learned at Framingham but
also found herself turning to the spirituals she had played
as a child. Booker was her best audience and severest critic.
His taste in music ran to the classics, even though publicly
he was a great advocate of Negro spirituals. But because of
his frequent trips, Portia was left mostly alone with her
piano. Her Framingham training put her beyond the musical training available at Tuskegee and she found little intellectual challenge in her course work. She felt as if she were
treading water until her father turned a hand to her destiny
yet another time.

Booker had recently engaged a certain Professor Talley.

Talley came from Hampton Institute where he had been a teacher of mathematics and German. Lured to Tuskegee under the guise of teaching the former, he soon found that his real merit to his employer resided in his knowledge of German. In his autobiography Booker wrote, "I remember that the first coloured man whom I saw who knew something about foreign languages impressed me at the time as being a man of all others to be envied."

Each evening Portia now found herself at the home of Professor Talley and his wife, receiving instruction in the German language. She remembered being mystified by this new turn of events but welcomed it as a break in the mind-dulling routine of dressmaking. The Latin that had been part of her course of study at Framingham equipped her with some foundation in language learning and being "bright as a piranha" (Booker's wry description), she progressed rapidly. "Pa always had a plan for me," Portia felt, "and there he was getting me ready for it and I didn't even know it!"

It is not known if "the plan" was even clear to Booker in the beginning, but it was probably related to a communiqué he received from the German Embassy in Washington around the turn of the century. The German Colonial Society had proposed that an expedition of Tuskegee graduates be sent to their colony Togoland (later, Togo) to teach the Africans modern methods of cotton production. Such a venture was undertaken but encountered great difficulties and eventually floundered on the continent whose West Coast climate is historically inhospitable to Westerners. In the meantime, lines of communication became established between Tuskegee and Germany that were to directly bear upon Portia's future. As Portia saw it, ". . . to show you how smart he [Booker] was, he always kept his plans in the back of his head, never revealing them, especially to white people, until they were ripe."

Portia could not have made a more insightful observation of Booker T. Washington the man. By the end of the nineteenth century, Booker had forged a major institution whose reputation and influence reached far beyond the borders of its campus. The student body numbered over a thousand and the faculty of some one hundred conducted their classes in modern brick buildings. The Atlanta speech of September 1895 had swung wide the gates of white philanthropy. New England was still being cultivated, but it was on the industrial north that Tuskegee now focused its main attention.

To such men as Andrew Carnegie and John D. Rockefeller the Tuskegee vocational philosophy made sense. They along with other industrialists such as William H. Baldwin, Sr., assumed places on Booker's board of trustees formerly held by New England clergymen. With each new wealthy contact, Booker schemed to be introduced to yet another one. Once he had secured a potential donor's interest, he arranged for him or her to visit the campus. Portia was briefly introduced to many of these wealthy people, but her most vivid recollection was that of falling asleep to the sound of the Tuskegee choral group singing late into the night the Negro spirituals that Booker's guest of the moment always seemed to request.

Even with the diversions provided by visitors, music, and language lessons, Portia found herself chafing under the narrow strictures of Tuskegee life. In the fall of 1901, she enrolled in Wellesley College in Massachusetts. Upon reflecting on this period in her life a note of bitterness crept into Portia's voice. She had been formally educated only through the lower grades of secondary school and, therefore, was admitted as a special student to concentrate on music and German. Because of pressure exerted by the parents of southern students, she was denied living quarters in the college dormitories. Rebuffed but still undaunted, she took up residency in an off-campus boardinghouse run by a Mrs. B. H. Brehaut.

Portia threw herself into her music, employing it yet another time to stave off loneliness. She credits her teacher, a Miss Hurd, with providing her fine training, but Wellesley as a school did not emphasize music. In her isolation from normal campus life, Portia grew despondent. Her grades fell in her other subjects and, at the end of the school year, she voluntarily withdrew. It seems Portia was to be damned if she did and damned if she didn't. She returned to Tuskegee to find herself greatly criticized for having dropped out. But Portia refused to be rebuked: "I went to Wellesley, which I had no business doing. I wasn't prepared for college . . . people said some very unkind things about me . . . but they didn't realize that that was just a resting place until I got ready to go somewhere."

After the loneliness of Wellesley, she was happy to be back at The Oaks with her family. She resumed her station at the piano in the parlor, showing off her increased skill to her father who would listen while at work in his study. Even though Portia and Maggie had called a truce, Booker was always to stand at the center of his daughter's love. In reflecting on her relationship with her stepmother, Portia said, "It wasn't exactly a reconciliation. I loved her in a way, because she was so kind to my father and to the students. And I realized that she'd never had children, and she couldn't know that my desire for love and tenderness was something that my father could fill, but she couldn't."

As much as Booker would have wanted his home situation different, he recognized that Portia had to be firmly launched on a separate life of her own. For the further growth and musical development of the spirited child he had fathered, Tuskegee was a dead end. So with his encouragement and help, the restless Portia began to take steps to secure her release. She devoured ads in newspapers and magazines, writing for catalogues to schools all over the country. By a careful process of elimination, they finally fixed upon Bradford Academy in Bradford, Massachusetts.

Bradford Academy had a strong music department and was located not far from Boston, Booker's northern base. It was an exclusive five-year private school for young ladies of the better classes. Founded in 1803, Bradford was a prototypic New England institution which produced graduates imbued with the Yankee tradition. The school also had a long standing policy of not admitting Negroes or Jews.

Had Portia been the daughter of an ordinary black man, this "gentlemen's agreement" would have remained intact. But Booker T. Washington had not earned the appellative of the "wizard" to have his daughter's ambitions thwarted at this juncture. Over the years he had painstakingly forged an intricate network of influential contacts and associations that afforded him seemingly endless power. A large block of that power was concentrated in the board of trustees he had marshaled for Tuskegee. A member of the board, Alice Freeman Palmer, also sat as trustee for Bradford Academy. Booker's daughter was summarily admitted with no further questions raised. Consistent with the Booker Washington image, integration was not the issue; no racial barricades had been broken for there was not to be another black graduate of Bradford until 1919. Booker just wanted the best for his Portia; Tuskegee would provide for the masses.

After Wellesley, Portia approached Bradford with some trepidation. She was determined to make it this time but had her guard up against the racial discrimination she expected to encounter. She was old enough now, in 1902, to be aware of the storm of controversy that ebbed and flowed around her father. All whites did not hold him in esteem, she had learned, and therefore his ability to protect his daughter was not invincible.

Her first days on campus were uneventful. True, she was placed in the only single room in the dormitory but she had expected that. She was prepared to keep to herself, loneliness not being an unfamiliar state to her. But gradually, in small groups, her fellow students came to her door or sought her out after class. By nature Portia was very social and, though fearful, she could not resist the overtures being made to her. They touched her brown skin and, with surprise, the wavy hair that was as soft as their own. For the most part, these wealthy young white girls had never known a Negro but had grown up on the abolitionist tradition of their Yankee parents and cried over *Uncle Tom's Cabin*. To them, Portia defied the stereotype and in her uniqueness became a prized friend to have. "They worshiped me," Portia warmly remembered. "I was something different and I liked that." Race, rather than a handicap this time, worked to her advantage.

She plunged wholeheartedly into campus life, being elected an officer of the student government association in her second year. No token appointment, Portia took her duties very seriously, even to arranging with her father to have the association's records printed up. The acceptance and warmth that she encountered released her natural high spiritedness and good humor in such a manner that she was truly happy for the first time in a long while.

When her musical talents became known, she graciously consented to play for the morning chapel exercises and the school dances. She was also the accompanist for the Mandolin Club and performed with them in concerts at Boston's

Hotel Vendome. Her formal training was overseen by a talented piano master, Professor Samuel Morse Downes.

From the beginning Downes expressed great enthusiasm for Portia's musical talent. He seems to have gone out of his way to encourage her development. After the drab years at Tuskegee, Portia blossomed under this attention and advanced rapidly in her skill at the piano. Her progress confirmed Downes's initial feeling about his pupil's potential. On the strength of his recommendation, Bradford Academy awarded Portia a music scholarship midway through her first year. This grant assured her the concentrated piano training which she craved but could not have otherwise afforded at Bradford.

Unfortunately, the rest of Portia's financial situation was not so comfortable. Although she received a monthly allowance from home, she always seemed to be broke and slightly in debt. Portia borrowed money from her classmates and made purchases at the local stores on credit. Booker, from whom she hid nothing, reprimanded her in his letters for borrowing or running up bills she had not cleared with him in advance.

But Portia seemed incapable of living on an allowance and her letters always included a plea for a little extra money. Surrounded by girls from wealthy families and steeped in her pride as Booker T. Washington's daughter, Portia felt she had to keep up the best of appearances. She wrote to her father that she felt "shabby" in the homemade Tuskegee clothes that had come to be an embarrassment to her. Even though she roomed alone, her quarters had to be as nicely appointed as any others in the dormitory, hence a request in another letter for money to purchase a new wastepaper basket. She even pleaded for traveling money so as to appear as carefree as her classmates in going off on day trips to Boston. Maggie and Booker thought the clothes and money they sent more than adequate for their daughter's personal needs. But Portia could no longer live within these limited means. She had come to embrace a richer world than the one she had left behind in Alabama.

The Oaks had been a large comfortable home in which to grow up, but life there was staidly conducted and with few frills. Both Booker and Maggie maintained Spartan regimen in their personal lives, to which Portia and her brothers also had to conform. One rose early in the Washington household, to begin a day entirely devoted to industrious activity. When home and not at work in his study, Booker prowled the campus, taking note of anything he deemed awry, from a sagging gate to a casually dressed student. One of the few pleasures he allowed himself was working in his vegetable garden or slopping the pigs he regarded as the mainstay of the southern black's diet. Maggie went early to her office, from where she ruled the lives of the female students down to the last detail. The Washington children, when not in school, had regular chores to do around the house, after which they were allowed to quietly play in the yard until dinnertime.

When there were guests, which was often, the children took their meals in the kitchen, after the manner of the Victorian age which held that children were seen, briefly, and heard not at all. Even when only the family was in attendance, dinner was a formal affair prepared and served by students from the housekeeping department. Booker, still in starched collar and tie, would quietly listen as each of his children recited his or her activities for the day. Mr. Washington and Mrs. Washington, as they were wont to address each other except when alone, confined their exchanges to generalities, mindful of the alert ears of their student servants. The family might then assemble in the living room where Booker would read aloud from the Bible or Portia would play the piano until bedtime.

This comfortable, if sterile, life style was made possible by Booker's success in attracting large donors to the Institute who insisted that the founder be well provided for. By 1901 the school's property was valued at over $300,000 and, in addition to Carnegie and Rockefeller, Booker counted the financial giants Collis P. Huntington, George Foster Peabody, and William E. Dodge among Tuskegee's staunchest supporters. President William McKinley had become, in 1898, the first of four United States Presidents to eventually visit the campus.

With such men in close attendance upon her father, Portia could not be blamed for her disregard of sound money management. The Washington family lived well and there always seemed to be another contributor around the corner to support the continuing expansion of the Institute.

Portia's belief in her father was so complete that she could not conceive of a time in which money would not be ultimately forthcoming. Tragically, Booker had passed on to his daughter a philanthropy-dependent mentality about finances that was to plague her the rest of her life.

In spite of money problems, the years spent at Bradford were rewarding ones for Portia. Between extracurricular activities, piano lessons, and her course work, she was in constant motion. With the exception of "gymnasium work," she did very well in her studies, earning As and Bs. Her dedication was to finally take its toll when, in March of her junior year, she landed in the school infirmary with a bad cold and an ulcerated tooth. She wrote to her father of her misery and he arranged for her to pass the coming Easter holiday resting up with friends in New York City.

Booker was spending increasing amounts of time in the Empire City and would shortly shift his northern base there to be closer to the wealthy industrialists he now courted. New York was also rapidly becoming the spiritual capital of black America, as large numbers of blacks moved into the Manhattan neighborhood known as Harlem. The "Harlem Renaissance" still lay in the future, but already this community had begun to attract the brightest and most talented blacks of the time. The ever-shrewd Booker moved to coalesce this potential black power with his towering presence. Many northern, more urbane blacks had little regard for the Washington policy, but, in spite of their aloofness, they were to still feel his power. Covertly, as was his style, the "Fox" prevailed upon his moneyed white backers to provide the capital needed by certain black business ventures and publications concerned with black advancement, thus giving Booker a controlling voice in their operation.

Portia knew nothing of these behind-the-scenes machinations. What she remembered was that "Pa loved New York" and how she loved being part of the excitement that surrounded him during his business trips there. Restored in health and replenished in spirit, she returned to Bradford to finish out the school year. The summer of 1904 found her at Weymouth, Massachusetts, where the Washington family gathered at the summer home lent to them by William Baldwin. Portia recalled little of that summer because her thoughts were on returning to Bradford as a senior. At the end of September, she would write to her father, "This year is going to be a very busy one with me though not so hard as previous years have been . . . I am in splendid health now —never felt better. I sleep better than ever before."

She selected a course of study at Bradford that included composition, English literature, evolution of Christianity, Bible, and music. Especially exciting to her was the prospect of her senior thesis. Predictably, it was entitled "The Mission of the American Negro." As an emissary of the Washington philosophy, Booker could not have found another so loyal. She even wrote to him requesting "good," i.e., pro-Washington, black newspapers that would support her in proselytizing her classmates. There was a Boston newspaper, *The Guardian*, that was openly attacking her father and his policies. Published by William Monroe Trotter, it was about the only black newspaper Booker could not control or silence. Trotter was the complete antithesis of Booker T. Washington in both background and philosophy. Born in Ohio, April 7, 1872, and raised in the Boston suburb of Hyde Park, Trotter had been graduated from Harvard University in 1895 as the first black elected to its Phi Beta Kappa chapter. Raised in moderate wealth and comfort, Trotter early came to a belief in the intellectual ability of blacks to succeed if freed of the racist barriers imposed by American society. He scoffed at Booker's anti-integrationist philosophy of vocational training and, with the launching of his newspaper, *The Guardian,* in 1901, set out systematically to challenge the older race leader in his weekly editorials. A man of some means, Trotter could not be influenced as others had been by Booker's patronage and influence with rich whites. Portia had a particular reason to dislike Trotter as he had published the fact that she had flunked out of Wellesley, writing that Booker T. Washington's children "are not taking to higher education like a duck to water, and while their defect in this line is doubtless somewhat inherited, they justify to some extent their father's well-known antipathy to anything higher than the three Rs for his 'people.'" With Boston's proximity to Bradford, Portia sought any ammunition available to counteract adverse publicity against her father and to settle the score with Trotter for herself.

But Booker's hold on his white New England constituency was firm. In December 1904 he visited Bradford for a short speech after the evening's chapel service. A month earlier he had completed a successful speaking engagement at the Abbot Academy for girls in nearby Andover. On this occasion Portia organized a group to attend his speech at Bradford's rival school and listened with knowing pride as her father enthralled yet another audience.

But Booker was not always to be in total control of the circumstances surrounding his public appearances. His daughter sanguinely recalled one occasion when she journeyed down from Bradford to hear him speak before a large black audience assembled in a Boston church. It was a rare appearance for Booker. He seldom spoke to large gatherings of blacks outside of the South. Trotter and his *Guardian* editor, George Forbes, had worked out a plan to heckle Booker into discrediting himself by revealing what in their opinion was his "Uncle Tom" attitude toward black suffrage and education.

Every seat in the church was filled, Portia remembered, and the audience was electric with anticipation of the rumored confrontation. As she seated herself near the podium, Portia's senses tingled with the unfolding drama. Outwardly, she remained calm, steeled by her infinite faith in her father. But she was nervous about the masses of flowers that bedecked the church. She was convinced that the flowers had been deliberately placed to induce an unnerving sneezing fit in her father; another contemporary account reported sneezing powder being thrown from the balcony for this purpose.

In any event, her fears soon abated when, calmly assuming the rostrum, Booker quickly and easily cast his famous oratorical spell over the audience. With each wave of enthusiastic applause, Portia settled back to enjoy the now familiar spectacle. But she was snapped to attention by the dissonant voice of Monroe Trotter challenging Booker from the floor. Refusing to be threatened, Booker ignored or parried

The Guardian publisher, point for point. Portia writhed in her seat, wanting to reach up and smash this man attempting to humiliate her father. But Booker refused to yield an inch to his adversary even though Trotter proved equally as tenacious. The church was in an uproar, which the newspapers exaggerated into near-riot proportions. The police were summoned and Trotter, with great protest, was hauled off to jail. Afterward Portia remembered laughing with her father who considered the whole thing a big joke.

But, it was hardly a laughing matter to Dr. W. E. B. Du Bois. A number of years had passed since Portia had been introduced to the then-recent Harvard graduate when she had come down to Boston from Framingham to hear her father speak. Since that time, Du Bois had established a reputation as one of the brightest of the new black intellectuals who opposed the Booker Washington political and social doctrines. While not always in total agreement with the more radical Trotter, Du Bois became incensed by the Boston affair and Booker's naked use of power to stifle legal rights of dissent.

As the direct result of this incident, Du Bois sent out a call "for organized determination and aggressive action on the part of men who believe in Negro freedom and growth." In response, a group of twenty-nine men representing fourteen states came together at Niagara Falls, Canada, in June 1905 to form what came to be known as the "Niagara Movement." In Du Bois' words, they committed themselves "to oppose firmly present methods of strangling honest criticism; to organize intelligent and honest Negroes; and to support organs of news and public opinion" as a necessary alternative to the Washington program. Five years later the National Association for the Advancement of Colored People (NAACP) would become the first major organized challenge to the Booker T. Washington empire.

Although Portia was aware of the rising furor surrounding her father, he saw to it that she was carefully sheltered from its full impact. Bradford was geographically and psychologically removed from the mainstream of black life. From the time of her enrollment there, Booker had discouraged Portia from fraternizing with people of color other than those he had selected. For example, Portia had wanted to spend one of her school holidays in New York City at a Harlem boardinghouse. Her father flatly refused the request and only allowed her visit to the city after he arranged for her lodging with a "respectable" black family of his acquaintance in Brooklyn.

Booker even went so far in his vigilance as to provide Portia with whatever male companionship she experienced in her college years. Emmett J. Scott, her father's most devoted and trusted secretary, came often to Boston on Tuskegee business. Dutifully, he would call upon Portia and escort her into the city for concerts and the theater. Portia remembered liking Scott, whereas most of her other carefully screened dates were uninteresting. Because she loved any opportunity to be out on the town, she accepted dates even with the dullest of these men. In retrospect, she felt that she did not really miss the social life enjoyed by her peers because she devoted most of her time and thought to music.

Her senior year raced by with the acceleration that always seems to occur when an era in one's life draws toward a close. Already Portia was looking forward to graduation and the possible next step in the "plan." At the start of her last year she wrote to her father:

October 23, 1904

My dearest papa:

I was so glad to get your letter and the music. I suppose you are very tired after the busy time you had north. I keep up with you . . .

School is going nicely—We keep busy every single minute and while I really love Bradford—I shall not be sorry when I graduate because of the nervous strain—I feel—nearly all the time.

Last Saturday night we had a mock campaign and Mr. [Theodore] Roosevelt was elected 81 to 12. We Republicans had a long procession with [Democratic nominee Alton B.] Parker in effigy born on pall—it was surely fun.

One of the teachers here is getting up a party to go abroad, next summer, and is very anxious to have me in her party. It is to cost about four hundred dollars. What do you think of this? I hope that Miss [Jane Ethel] Clark can go too. I have written her about it . . .

> With lots of love—
> I am your daughter
> Portia

Booker thought a trip to Europe a very good idea. He and Maggie had traveled the Continent in 1898 and knew how broadening the experience would be for their daughter. It would have appealed anyway to the snob in Booker because it was an age in which all young ladies of culture were expected to take the Grand Tour. The presence of Miss Clark, an assistant principal at Tuskegee and Portia's friend, would complete the picture by providing the proper traveling companion and chaperone.

As the school year progressed, the plan for Europe assumed larger proportions. Professor Downes pressed Portia to consider a serious future in music. He believed her very talented but in need of concentrated training in the technique he had received as a student. Downes had studied in Berlin with a great teacher named Martin Krause. When contacted, Krause agreed to see Portia but only because of the professor's strong recommendation.

Portia

In the beginning, Portia was overwhelmed by the possibility of study in a foreign country. But always quick to move onto something new and becoming increasingly more excited at the prospects of truly being on her own, she pushed the proposal with her family. Booker gradually warmed to his daughter's enthusiasm. He knew there would be few opportunities in the United States for his daughter on the scale befitting the Washington name. Reports that he had received about Germany in those pre-Nazi days indicated that blacks were more readily accepted in the larger society there. He was further reassured by his continuing contact with the German Colonial Society and with the enthusiastic reception his autobiography had received when published there in 1902.

With Booker's concurrence, Portia's trip came closer to being a reality. There were many details to be worked out and as late as May 1905 Portia was still making up her mind about living in a boarding school or with a German family. Booker and her German teacher at Bradford urged the latter, which Portia, perhaps remembering her loneliness at Framingham, finally also accepted. The only obstacle now, as always, was money. But Booker successfully prevailed upon his white benefactor Andrew Carnegie for the money and in June 1905, Portia Washington set sail for Europe.

3

Free, Black, and over Twenty-one

Portia sailed almost immediately after graduation and, as originally planned, she was accompanied by Jane Ethel Clark, who was a graduate of Oberlin College and an assistant principal at Tuskegee. Highly regarded by Booker T. Washington, she often was called upon to travel as Tuskegee's emissary. Now he had entrusted her with her most important assignment, as chaperone and companion to his daughter.

Their crossing was quite pleasant, Portia recalled, with mild weather, delicious new foods, and fellow passengers who, though aloof, were civil. Both Portia and Jane were light brown in complexion and were assumed to be East Indians. But one white southern woman, aghast at the proximity of "nigras," refused at first to sit in the same dining room. When apprised of who they were, she could not get close enough to them at the table, positively gushing with praise for Booker T. Washington.

Such occurrences were to be a familiar scene to Portia, but Booker's fame coupled with her increasing maturity gave her a confidence and poise that would enable her to cope with prejudice. More often than not, she would sit back and wait with good humor the comeuppance that bigoted white people inevitably received from the power invoked by her father's name. But even in those few instances

55

where this formula failed, she was unshaken because of her own sense of self-worth and in-born feistiness.

They disembarked in England with plans to travel on the Continent for the summer, arriving in Berlin just in time for the fall. They sought lodging in a London boardinghouse which Booker had recommended to Portia while she was still at Bradford. The Washingtons had stayed at this particular place during their European tour and recalled that it was located in a very good section of the city. "The Prince and Princess of Wales drove by the house one morning, . . ." Booker recalled in his letter to Portia. "Of course it may have changed hands, but I rather suspect that it is still a boarding house." Booker did not know how prophetic his letter was to be. Portia and Jane had barely settled in when they were joined by other tourists whose speech clearly marked them as Southerners. Outraged by the presence of blacks, the newcomers demanded that they be put out. The landlady, though professing respect for their obvious respectability, asked Portia and Jane to leave.

Upon hearing of the incident, English friends of Booker quickly arranged for the evicted pair to stay in a private home. The London press picked up on the story, causing a small tremor of outrage among a liberal segment of the British gentry. Portia received a note of apology from the now humbled landlady, but this misfortune was after all to be a boon. Their hostess proved to be a lady of the English court and through her mansion passed many of the leading members of the aristocracy. Some came out of curiosity to meet black Americans for the first time, but most came to welcome the daughter of a man they greatly admired. Booker's work at Tuskegee had been closely studied by the British because of the similarities which existed, they believed, between the rural American south and colonial Africa and the West Indies. Booker, himself, had greatly impressed London society, speaking before a number of illustrious groups and even taking tea with the late Queen Victoria. Many of these people now sought out Portia with invitations to a busy round of receptions and dinner parties.

Portia loved every minute of her stay in London. She recalled with fondness the many friends that she made there, especially the T. Fisher Unwins. Mrs. Unwin, like Portia, was the daughter of a famous man, Richard Cobden, the English statesman. She and her husband had entertained Booker during his travels in England and now took it upon themselves to look after Portia. They arranged for Portia and Jane to stay in a new boardinghouse where it was guaranteed that there would be no unpleasant incidents.

Once comfortably lodged, Portia and Jane set out to explore the city. Booker had charged Jane with the responsibility of seeing to his daughter's educational enrichment as well as her social broadening. Dutifully, Portia accompanied Jane to the museums and historic sites that were a must for every American tourist. The livelier side of Portia's nature was released by evenings spent at the theater and music halls. Though somewhat staid, Jane allowed these diversions because she knew her employer would not object. (Just that summer Booker had invited the famous black American musical comedy team of Burt Williams and George Walker to entertain at the Washington retreat in Weymouth.) Portia really came alive at the theater, becoming almost intoxicated by the music and the elegance of the London audience. But Portia was always to be people-oriented and measured her life not in events but, rather, in terms of the people she had known. For her, the high point of London was meeting the famous black British composer Samuel Coleridge-Taylor.

Coleridge-Taylor was by this time at the height of his fame as a composer of operatic choral works. He had recently returned from a highly successful tour of the United States which included an invitation to the White House from the newly re-elected President, Theodore Roosevelt.

Humbly born in 1875 as the son of a ne'er-do-well medical practitioner from Sierre Leone, Samuel had been raised by his British mother in the quiet environs of Croydon, England. He early displayed a musical precociousness, which flowered into genius under the sensitive nuturing of several white mentors. By 1905 he was the conductor of the Croydon Conservatory, the Westmorland Festival, the Rochester Choral Society, and the Croydon Orchestral Society and held a professorship of composition at the Trinity College of Music in London.

He had gained immediate fame with the performance of his choral composition, *Hiawatha,* and by the turn of the century was well known throughout American musical circles. He traveled to the United States in 1904 under the aegis of the Samuel Coleridge-Taylor Society of Washington, D.C. A two-hundred-voice chorus, this group was remarkable for the times because it had been entirely conceived, trained, and financed by black people. Their inspiring performance of *Hiawatha* launched Samuel on a concert tour before integrated audiences throughout the United States.

It was in Boston that Samuel first encountered Portia's father. At breakfast in the home of a black family named Lee, Samuel expressed admiration for the work Booker was doing in the South. However, he had been sent a copy of W. E. B. Du Bois' *The Souls of Black Folks* some months earlier and had written to a friend that it was "the greatest book he had ever read." He could not help but take exception with Booker's emphasis on manual training to the exclusion of the development of black people on an intellectual and artistic

A Tuskegee dressmaking class, in 1906, of the type in which Portia reluctantly enrolled before college. *Library of Congress*

The Tuskegee Faculty Council, 1902. *First row, left to right:* Jane E. Clark, Emmett J. Scott, BTW, Warren Logan, John H. Washington. *Second row:* R. R. Taylor, R. M. Attwell, Major Julius Ramsey, E. J. Penney, M. T. Driver, William Maberry, George Washington Carver. *The Francis Benjamin Johnston Collection, Library of Congress*

Above, Portia (*first right, middle row*), c. 1904, and the Bradford Academy Mandolin Club, for which she was the piano accompanist.
Al Hall, Bradford College

Left, Portia's graduation portrait, Bradford Academy, Bradford, Massachusetts, Class of '05.
Al Hall, Bradford College

Left, Abbie Mitchell, in 1902, a singer and actress whose successful fortunes also led her to Berlin. *Schomburg Center, The New York Public Library, Astor, Lenox and Tilden Foundations*

Right, Samuel Coleridge-Taylor, c. 1908, British composer of African descent whose music secured Portia the gay life in Europe. *Schomburg Center, The New York Public Library, Astor, Lenox and Tilden Foundations*

Booker T. Washington, c. 1910, the "Moses of his people,"
at the peak of his power. *Schomburg Center, The New York
Public Library, Astor, Lenox and Tilden Foundations*

Booker T. Washington, in 1915, astride his favorite mount
the same year as his death. *Library of Congress*

level. It can only be imagined that a spirited yet polite discussion ensued. Samuel probably admitted his debt to Booker's South because of the influence the Fisk Jubilee Singers had had on his composing of *Hiawatha* after hearing them during their European tour some years before. Besides, Samuel looked to the poet Paul Laurence Dunbar as an inspiration and Dunbar, because of his close friendship with Booker, had written the Tuskegee school song.

By the time Samuel completed his 1904 tour of America, he was to feel greater respect for the Booker Washington doctrine. To an interviewer upon his return to England, he was quoted as saying, "As soon as people found out I was English they were quite different. Of course, at first they could not reconcile the absence of the Yankee twang in a man of colour like myself. At the same time, I was sorry for coloured people generally. I heard some pitiful stories about their treatment. I met a young coloured lady of great educational attainments and of refined tastes. She was travelling south of Washington, and was turned out of the car. Coloured people and white are separated when travelling on the other side of a line drawn south of Washington. In the car for coloured passengers a hulking lounger wiped his feet on the hair of her head. Other indignities, too, were perpetrated, for which there was absolutely no redress. Think of it, if the aggrieved parties were whites! When I go to Tuskegee, it will be in Mr. Booker Washington's own private car, and consequently I shall avoid being insulted. What is so deplorable to me is that there is as yet very little discrimination between the educated and decent-minded black and the idle and semi-civilised man of colour. This, understand me, is from an English point of view. The fact is, no Englishman can get quite inside the question, it is really so subtle."

Samuel did not get to make that trip to Tuskegee but found himself instead entertaining the founder's daughter in his own home in Croydon a year later. Portia was quite nervous about meeting the man whose arrangements of Negro spirituals she had grown up loving. But Samuel was a gentle, unassuming person who, along with his wife and young children, Hiawatha and Gwendolyn, quickly put Portia at ease. She was flattered when he asked her to play one of his pieces but Portia declined, promising instead to play for him after she had gained a better technique in Germany. Portia was not often modest, but when it came to a professional judgment of her music, she was always to be very exacting of herself. Samuel understood this quality and did not press her. Besides, he wanted to hear about her plans for Berlin, enjoying as he did, according to his biographer, conversation, coffee, and cigarettes almost as much as music. To study in Germany had been his long-time dream. Though he was never to realize it, he mastered the language and was to engage Portia in animated German conversations thereafter when they met.

By midsummer, Portia and her chaperone had taken leave of London and journeyed to Paris. Not knowing the language, Portia found the French capital somewhat bewildering. It was a curious fact that as a child she had taken immediately to German but hated French and could never master it. Luckily, Jane was fairly proficient in French and quickly got them settled. Booker had visited Paris and, although well received by the French, he had come away with a very disapproving opinion of French "morality and moral earnestness." But he knew that his daughter's European education would not be complete without exposure to the cultural attributes of the City of Light. Besides, he had chosen well in Jane Clark who as a vigilant guardian would write from Paris, "I am very glad that I live in a country where standards are different from those here."

Even with this prudishness, there were to be fun times in their visit. In a somewhat lighter vein, Jane reported to Booker that, "There are several colored men connected with the American Embassy here and they have been very generous in piloting us around. . . . We are having very glorious days—such gay, fascinating ones."

One of the best times remembered by Portia was their encounter with Dr. Edward W. Blyden. "We spent the evening at the Hotel des Champs Élysées," Jane wrote Booker, "as the guests of Dr. Blyden, Minister from Liberia to France, Germany and the Court of St. James's. This hotel is the most magnificent one I have ever seen. Many people from the various embassies stop here. The [Shah] of Persia with his retinue of sixty men and eighty servants was also a guest at the hotel . . . It was a glorious evening! I was especially glad to see Dr. Blyden . . . He seems like a dear old man. He is going to take us sight-seeing Saturday afternoon. He sails for America next month and says he is coming South—mainly to see Tuskegee."

Portia was flying high, secretly enjoying every minute of the "wickedness" she was allowed to glimpse. But the swiftness of Paris life began to wear on Jane and on August 2, 1905, she wrote Booker of her longing "for more quiet regions." A week after the Blyden party, she bundled Portia up and booked them both on a train to Switzerland. Because the summer was nearly over, it was time to rest and prepare for the serious business awaiting them in Berlin.

The leaves had begun to turn when they arrived in the German capital. Portia was struck by the beauty of the city and the same crispness in the air that she had come to love in New England. She had been seasoned by her travels and felt herself wiser in the ways of the larger world. Her confidence was buoyed by her familiarity with the German language and all that she had been enthusiastically told about Berlin by her "dear Professor Downes" at Bradford. Secretly, her greatest source of self-satisfaction was the anticipation of being on her own for the first time in her life. Jane was scheduled to return soon to Tuskegee for the opening of the fall term. Though Portia had been away from home nearly half of her life, it had always been in the company of adults selected by her father. Now, even though she was fond of Jane and would miss her, she was eager to be completely independent and on her own.

Her freedom was still contingent on her acceptance as a student by the teacher she had been sent to Berlin to meet. Martin Krause had been a pupil of Franz Liszt and had succeeded the master composer as a highly esteemed pianist in his own right. Only the most promising of students were taken under his instruction and Portia's Professor Downes had been one of his best. He agreed to see Portia because of Downes's strong recommendation and, possibly, because of his knowledge of Booker T. Washington.

The day of the audition Portia arose early and practiced several hours on the piano in the parlor of the boarding-house where she and Jane had secured lodging. She ran through her repertoire of Bach, Beethoven, and Chopin in quick succession and then set the sheets of this music aside. That part of her practicing had been merely a warm-up, for Portia had no intention of attempting the classics with a student of Liszt. Downes had been very candid in his estimate of the limited quality of her classical technique. Trusting his judgment, Portia had decided upon a daring plan of action even before leaving the United States. She would audition with the music she knew best, Negro spirituals, and in particular the one she loved most, "Sometimes I Feel Like a Motherless Child." With a silent prayer to Samuel Coleridge-Taylor whose arrangement she planned to use, she and Jane set out for the great maestro's studio.

Krause received her politely and, after a few warm-up exercises and an encouraging nod from Jane, Portia launched into "Motherless Child." Krause was amazed at what he heard, bouncing up out of his seat and spouting a stream of German accolades as he rushed to her side at the piano. Startled by his enthusiastic response, Portia became shy at her daring but in halting German she tried to explain the meaning of the spiritual to black people and this particular one to her personally. He listened intently as she talked and played additional selections to illustrate her point. The long audition finally came to an end with a thoroughly enthralled Herr Krause eager to begin work with his new student.

The following summer, Portia was to tell Samuel Coleridge-Taylor of her success with his song and she remembered that "he was tickled to death to know that I had played his work for this famous teacher and was accepted on it . . . He became my friend."

Portia's year of study was now secure. Jane prepared to return to America, eager to report firsthand to her employer how successful his daughter had been. Before departing, she arranged for Portia to live in a boardinghouse more convenient to Krause's studio and frequented by other students. Having herself been one of the first black students at Oberlin College, Jane remembered her easier acceptance by her white student peers than by the society at large.

With Jane's departure, Portia joyfully set about ordering her new life. She arose each morning at 6:00 A.M. to practice on the piano she had secured for her use at the new boardinghouse. She usually put in two or three hours of playing before a bell would ring summoning the house residents to breakfast. At first Portia was the object of an ambivalent curiosity to her fellow boarders. Many of them were Americans who approached the dining table with mixed feelings about breaking bread with a black person. But, with a few exceptions, even the most reluctant were eventually won over by Portia's wit and their own willingness to be daring so far from home.

Her Berlin stay was to be perhaps the happiest period in Portia's life. For the first time she was able to immerse herself completely in her music. Krause assigned her to one of his advanced students, Henry Schmidt. An American, Schmidt was to later become head of the music department at a leading university in Pennsylvania. Portia met with him three times a week for lessons heavy in emphasis on technical work. Krause thought Portia very talented when he reviewed her work at the end of each month but constantly exhorted her to strengthen her technique. Determined to be successful—for herself, for her father, and for her race—Portia practiced from eight to ten hours daily. Often she would look up wondering where the day had gone and, with it, the evening meal hour.

Portia loved German food, finding it strong and substantial like the southern cooking on which she had been raised. Sometimes when she had worked late she would allow herself to be enticed by her more carefree fellow students out into the Berlin evening for a repast at a local *Brauhaus*. Flushing at the memory of long-past pleasures, Portia conjured up scenes reminiscent of *The Student Prince*. There was much singing and quaffing of beer, and the more playful elements of her personality were allowed release. Unknown to her father, such evenings came to be quite frequent occasions. In fact, Portia was to have more than a passing flirtation with the gay bohemian life of Berlin.

One of her evenings out she was approached by a well-dressed but not particularly distinguished-looking man. She had noticed him studying her from across the room and was intrigued enough to allow him to join her and her friends at their table. He was accompanied by another man who hovered in the background like a combination servant and chaperone. The stranger ignored his companion's obvious concern, fixing his full attention on Portia. He inquired as to what she was, to which Portia wryly responded, "Just an American studying music in Berlin." Before the evening was over, he had prevailed upon this witty lady to play for him. Always pleased to have an audience, Portia invited her new acquaintance and his shadow to her boardinghouse. She showed off at first with the classics, but soon launched into her beloved spirituals. Her guest was enthralled, staying late into the night, insisting on yet one more Negro song. Portia happily obliged until she was exhausted. With a gallant salute, her guests finally took their leave, singing her praises out into the dawning new day. Several days later, Portia received a note of appreciation that revealed her guests to be the son of the Kaiser and the bodyguard who always accompanied the heir apparent on his frequent incognito visits to the cafés of Berlin.

The discovery was thrilling, but Portia was not surprised that her visitor was an important personage. Whether inherited or picked up from Booker, she always seemed to have a way of connecting with the right people. She quickly sized up people, inevitably befriending those who were influential or talented. Portia was conscious of this knack and considered it correct in view of her famous heritage. As an artist, she felt licensed to have to associate only with other people who were also considered special. This snobbery in her character was probably unavoidable given the spoiling effects, especially her father's indulgences, during her childhood.

Officially, Portia's life in Berlin was under the guardianship of the German Colonial Society with which Booker had undertaken the Togoland venture. Portia was constantly turning to the Society for advances and loans between the checks that were sent from home. Just as at Bradford, money was available only in the form of a modest monthly allowance. The Washingtons lived comfortably but, still, little was left over for the kinds of extras that a girl in Portia's situation craved.

In 1903 Andrew Carnegie had offered Booker $600,000 for himself and his family. As Portia described it, Carnegie told her father, " 'Now Mr. Washington, you need to be comfortable, and you're doing such a great work. You're the Moses of your race. Here's a check for $600,000. This ought to take care of you and your family!' Booker T. looked at that check —I know I would—he looked at it but he said then, 'Oh, no, Mr. Carnegie, I can't accept that. Give it to Tuskegee, the boys and girls down there need an education and it would help them so much!' So, he wouldn't take it. Well at any rate, they later arranged for him to get a certain amount of the interest every month, you know. That and the home they gave him down there made him very comfortable. But when he [Booker] died he was poor as Job's turkey and even the interest didn't go to us."

Portia's month-to-month financial existence was no where more clearly spelled out than in a letter she received from her father soon after arriving in Berlin.

October 23, 1905

Miss Portia M. Washington
58 Steglitzer Strasse
Berlin, Germany

My dear Portia—
Enclosed I send you a memorandum showing the money which I have sent you during the last few months.

Your papa

Money sent Portia

June	(Berlin)	70.00
July	(Berlin)	70.00
Aug.	(London)	100.00
Sept.	(Berlin)	100.00
Oct.	(London)	40.00
		380.00

Amount Paid
Colonial Committee 90.00

470.00

Booker's attempts to be businesslike with Portia were destined to fail. His daughter seemed incapable of living within a modest budget. She recalled that she "would go down to the main German store and buy there anything I wanted. I didn't have any regard for money." Once a salesman told her that she was very extravagant and she laughingly replied, "Oh, I'm not, I just like nice things."

Portia's taste had begun to outstrip her resources even before she arrived in Berlin. Unknown to her father, she had borrowed money from the Colonial Society after exhausting the travel funds Booker had provided. He was quite miffed and wrote to her, "I have decided hereafter to put the whole matter of sending your money into the hands of your mother . . . she can attend to it more regularly and satisfactorily than I can." Probably feeling completely defeated, he also arranged for an account with the Colonial Society that would allow Portia to withdraw up to $100 for "urgent or unexpected needs." Even with these arrangements the improvident Portia would desperately cable later:

NO MONEY. FEBRUARY. CABLE. URGENT.

In April 1906 Portia spoke before a women's club in Berlin. She prepared very carefully for her appearance, even asking Booker to send her materials on which to base her speech. "Of course it will [be] a success," she wrote him. "*Think* whose daughter I am." Always her father's emissary, she was quick to respond to his request that she make herself available to several blacks of his acquaintance who would be traveling through Europe the summer of 1906, her second one abroad. One such visitor was John W. Robinson, who, with his wife, was en route to German West Africa to teach agriculture. His visit was especially welcome because he carried new clothes for Portia from Maggie.

The weather in Berlin was growing uncomfortably hot as Portia ended her first year of study. In terms of her music, the year had been a good one, but her exposure to the larger white world had not been without its problems. "I have had many unpleasant experiences in this boarding[house] this year," she wrote Booker, "but it is all good experience for me and I know human nature much better than ever before." She still had to take her final examination with Krause, but right after that she planned to get out of Berlin. Before departing she wrote to Booker of her activities.

68

Berlin
June 29—06

My dear father—

This is probably my last letter to you before I leave Berlin. I thought you would be interested to know how successful I was in my examination before Prof. Krause. He expressed himself as being much satisfied with my work and the great progress I have made during the year. He said that my work showed that I had been very industrious. I was so frightfully nervous over this examination that now I really am completely run down . . .

It is such a satisfaction for me to know that I have gained Prof. Krause's confidence and respect for he is one of the greatest teachers now living and his pupils are the best in Berlin . . .

Please write me. In care of the American Express Co. 3 Waterloo Pl. London.

I shall write you again when I get there.

Much love
Your Portia

Booker had wanted his daughter to stay close to Berlin, resting quietly somewhere in the countryside. Portia, however, was determined to get far away from Berlin and to a place where she had known only happiness. She promised to return to Berlin before the summer's end, but for now, London was her destination. She journeyed by train, dutifully noting to her father later that it had cost only $18 because she had taken the second-class coach. She arrived in London the morning of July 4, which, in a sense, she could claim as her personal Independence Day. There was no chaperone this time, and no studies or language barriers to slow her down.

She got in touch with many of the people who had welcomed her the previous summer, including the Unwins and Coleridge-Taylor. Her time was quickly filled with invitations, concerts, and sightseeing tours, so much so that the summer was over before she knew it. Before heading home, she made a short side trip to Scotland, saving the rest of Europe until the following summer when she would make the grand tour with her stepmother and half brother Ernest Davidson. Rested and refreshed, Portia returned to Berlin, eager to resume her studies.

All was not work, however, as earlier noted. Portia was twenty-three years of age and experienced in the vicissitudes of foreign living. She understood the German language nearly perfectly and was told that she spoke it almost as well. Though confident and sophisticated, Portia never forgot who she was, grabbing at any opportunity to touch a little bit of home. By necessity, her friends were white; by choice, they were mostly German. But the best friendship she was to make while in Berlin was to be with an American black woman, Abbie Mitchell.

Abbie Mitchell was a singer who had first gained fame in 1898 at the age of eighteen in the New York production of a tremendously popular black show, *Clorindy, or The Origins of the Cakewalk*. By the late 1890s, entirely black musical shows had begun to make their appearance in prominent American theaters. Prior to that time, the black image on the American stage had been the province of the black-faced white minstrel show. Through the creative genius of such men as Paul Laurence Dunbar, J. Rosamond Johnson, and Will Marion Cook, black theater transcended this condescending antecedent to become an innovative art form in its own right.

Will Marion Cook (the man Abbie was to eventually marry), produced an even more successful show, *In Da-*

homey, in 1902, which was invited to tour Europe. In England Abbie was singled out for special attention by the then Prince of Wales at a command performance of the *Dahomey* cast. A few years later, she was to return to Europe on her own for voice training in Paris and a concert tour of the major capitals.

Portia and Abbie became immediate friends during the singer's stop in Berlin. They were both about the same age, musically talented, and, most significantly, black women seeking success in a foreign land. Their friendship was to come full circle when, in 1931, Abbie went to Tuskegee Institute as the head of the vocal department.

The two young women were equally devoted to their music. They spent many happy hours at the piano, laughing and talking between bouts with the operatic music Abbie loved to sing. German lieder were her second love and Portia was helpful in perfecting her friend's accent. Portia also introduced her to the magnificent potential of traditional black music. The time would come when no concert given by Abbie Mitchell would be complete without a spiritual. The one most often chosen was "Sometimes I Feel Like a Motherless Child." Portia and Abbie said farewell to each other over a lavish dinner party given by Portia at one of the city's leading hotels. The gaiety of the evening softened the sadness of Abbie's departure but the friendship they established would be sustained many years into the future.

Most of Portia's social life in Berlin was kept carefully secret from her father. Victorian in his personal views, Booker would have looked upon some of his daughter's activities with disdain. Portia saw no harm in the gay evenings spent in the *Brauhaus* with the carefree students who had become her crowd. After the stern atmosphere of the Booker Washington household and the social sterility of her undergraduate days, it is no wonder that Portia embraced her new freedom with some abandon. She had inherited her mother's beauty, which combined with her witty and flirtatious personality to attract a coterie of suitors to her side. For the first time she was free to interact with men without the specter of her father hanging heavy over the relationships. While Portia's awakening womanhood reveled in this unbridled attention, she herself drew a line of demarcation, across which not even her most ardent pursuers were allowed. She could never forget whose daughter she was and the potentially scandalous consequences if she were discovered to be romantically involved with a white man. Thus Portia shied away from anything more personal with any one man than an evening out at the theater or concerts and then only with those whom she considered "very cultured." She admitted to having more than a passing flirtation with at least one of these men, but she cut the affair off when it became too serious. Even though Booker constantly consorted with white people, he kept his personal life and feelings rigidly segregated. Though young and romantic, Portia could not help but ultimately follow his example. He had given her opportunity but with responsibility, and she could not betray that trust. Besides, one breath of scandal would have had Portia summoned back to Tuskegee immediately.

Home seemed so far away to Portia as the first heady year abroad passed into a second one. She had maintained strong ties with her family through a steady stream of letters in which she reported on her studies and her official appearances at various functions as Booker T. Washington's daughter. She thought herself quite clever in keeping her two worlds apart, but midway through her second year this well-ordered arrangement was threatened with disruption. The cause of this new turn of events was a man she had met five years before coming to Berlin, William Sidney Pittman.

Sidney was a graduate of Tuskegee who had returned to teach at the school two years before Portia's ignominious return from Wellesley in 1902. He was a handsome and dynamic man who could not help but make a lasting impression on the then-nineteen-year-old Portia. They had first met on a day Sidney had been summoned to The Oaks to repair a mantel in one of the upstairs bedrooms. During his work, he was drawn downstairs by the sound of Portia practicing. "Oh my goodness," she remembered his saying, "you got some talent, girl." Portia was somewhat taken aback at first and did not quite know what to make of the striking Mr. Pittman. She was nearly eight years his junior and had had little experience with the opposite sex. But Sidney was persistent and her father did not disapprove, so she allowed herself to be swept into a courtship.

Their relationship was very proper, with Sidney coming to call on her at The Oaks, especially on Sunday evenings. Tuskegee had a ten-o'clock curfew, and even though Portia was not a regular student, Booker would call down from the head of the hall stairs, "Portia! Ten o'clock!" She remembered being so angry and Sidney quite annoyed, but they were at least permitted a final good-night kiss at the bottom of the porch steps. "My daddy would be up there looking, watching . . . he'd get a kick out of it really. He knew how he and Fanny had courted, and I don't suppose he left at any ten o'clock. Well, anyway, girls had to be straitlaced and he didn't want any criticism of me."

Sidney's intentions proved honorable and he presently informed Portia that he was going to marry her someday. Portia expressed skepticism, not because she did not care for him, but rather because she loved her music even more. She had made up her mind to pursue her studies and with her acceptance at Bradford Academy their relationship came to an end. But Sidney was not to forget his vow. Waiting perhaps for Portia to come of age and get her musical ambitions out of her system, Sidney moved to resume their courtship five years later. His efforts were to be aided by Portia's stepmother, Maggie, who had singled out Sidney almost from the beginning at Tuskegee for special attention. Sidney was a mulatto, and Maggie, also a mulatto, had great empathy for blacks of her complexion. Sadly, she knew all too well the rejection that light-skinned Negroes often experienced at the hands of both black and white people. She also came to view Sidney as quite brilliant, hard working, and, clearly, a good catch for her stepdaughter.

Booker liked and respected Sidney, but when apprised of the young man's intentions he expressed reluctance at his daughter's getting married at yet so early an age. He wanted her to remain in Berlin until she had completed the years of training necessary for her to be professionally self-sufficient. But under pressure from Maggie, he began to waver. Also, Portia felt, "at a certain time every man wants to see his daughter married. He feels safe when she's married. I imagine it was a responsibility having a daughter who had no mother." Maggie had tried to the best of her limited maternal instincts to succeed with her stepdaughter. Possibly she encouraged this match with a man Portia considered too old for herself in the hopes that it would alleviate Portia's dependence on her husband for constant love and affection.

Portia was flattered by the many letters she began to receive from Sidney. He had been her first beau and she remembered the excitement of the romantic feelings he had awakened in her then. But she was older and more experienced now and thought herself immune to former sentiments. "He wrote me these terrific love letters," Portia recalled. "Sometimes he'd put two in an envelope. He was dramatic—he knew how to get me." The letters were full of Sidney's ideas about being successful and taking care of Portia in the grand manner. He would also write about all the women who were after him. He must not have entirely discouraged this attention because one woman, the sister of one of Booker's secretaries, wrote Portia that Sidney was *her* boyfriend.

Sidney's mounting passion began to have its effect upon Portia, and she grew indecisive at the prospect of losing someone who seemed to cherish her so much. Berlin meant excitement and opportunity for artistic growth and personal freedom to her, but it also spelled alienation from the emotional security which she craved. The pressure from her stepmother compounded her dilemma, but with her father's acquiescence Portia found herself unable to resist Sidney any longer. The affair came to a head when Sidney issued a challenge that Portia could not refuse. "This is how clever he was," she recalled. "He wrote me a letter in Berlin [saying], 'Now it's going to be Halloween night or near there, or we'll just close it off and I'll marry somebody else!'" By return mail Portia accepted his proposal.

She was not entirely happy with her decision and the prospect of leaving Berlin, but she could not bring herself to give up Sidney. He loved her and promised that she could continue with her music. Her teachers were angered and begged her to reconsider, saying that she was giving up a brilliant musical future. Torn and troubled, Portia could only remember defending herself with "Every girl has to marry a good man when she can get him." Thoroughly defeated, Professor Krause refused to speak to her ever again.

Always the optimist, Portia squared her shoulders, conjured up romantic visions, and set sail for home to become Mrs. William Sidney Pittman, Halloween night, 1907.

4

Woman Alone

William Sidney Pittman was born in Montgomery, Alabama, April 21, 1875. His white father was unknown to him but was reputed to be a prominent resident of the city. Portia thought that this man, or perhaps his brother, was an architect whose talent Sidney was to inherit. Sidney's mother had been born a slave and upon emancipation became a laundress to support her family. Although there were other, older children in the family, Sidney seems to have been his mother's favorite. She encouraged him to complete public schools in both Montgomery and Birmingham. He was seventeen years old when he enrolled at Tuskegee, where he would work his way through the school for the next four years, graduating in 1897. He finished the basic education offered by the normal school but also received training in wheelwrighting, structural work, and architectual drawing. It is probable that during this time Sidney caught little more than a glimpse of Portia. She was still very much a child who led a sheltered, closely regulated life or was away at boarding school.

Booker looked with great favor on the new graduate, who appeared to be industrious, ambitious, intelligent, and a strong race man. Using money advanced by the school, Sidney went on for additional training in architecture and mechanical drawing at Drexel Institute in Philadelphia. He made such a favorable impression on his instructors there that he was granted a scholarship and received special mention upon graduating in 1900.

Despite his success, Sidney's experience at Drexel was not all smooth sailing. In appearance, he resembled his white antecedents more than his black ones. He was light complexioned, with dark wavy hair, and had features that could be described as strong but not necessarily Negroid. To further confound the prevailing stereotype of the southern Negro, he was well spoken, forthright, and extremely quick witted. A proud, arrogant man, Sidney would brook no insult to his dignity. One of his favorite stories, Portia remembered, was of the time a Drexel teacher made the mistake of saying something like "You know how your people are down south." Sidney bolted up in front of the class, demanding to know just which "people" he was talking about. Confronted with this angry white black man, the teacher retreated in apologetic confusion.

In 1900 Sidney returned to Tuskegee to work off his loan, a commitment the ever-shrewd Booker always extracted from students financed for education beyond his institution. Sidney was appointed head of the department of architectural drawing, with responsibility for the planning and supervision of all campus construction. Under his guidance more than a quarter million dollars' worth of construction was eventually completed, including a dormitory, library, and lecture hall. He also completed the plans and specifications for another one hundred fifty thousand dollars' worth of building in other parts of the South. It was during these early, successful days of his career at Tuskegee that the young architect encountered the president's daughter and determined upon the course that would make her his wife.

The wedding ceremony took place in the Tuskegee chapel. There was no great celebration but many relatives

and friends were in attendance. Portia remembered with
high amusement that her young cousins put bells under the
bed in which she spent her wedding night. Almost immediately, the new bride and groom boarded a train and headed
for Washington, D.C., where Sidney had been living for several years.

Sidney had resigned from Tuskegee in 1903 after a quar-
rel with the school's chief architect, Robert R. Taylor.
Booker refused to take sides in the argument, trying instead
to bring the two men together in the manner of compromise
at which he was so adept. Sidney had a hot-blooded nature
and refused to be conciliatory. He thought that he was un-
derpaid, underappreciated, and could go elsewhere and do
better. He set up an architectural office on Louisiana Avenue in downtown Washington. This was a bold move then,
given the highly segregated nature of the nation's capital.
But Sidney was as determined as he was brilliant. He refused to be told by anyone black or white where he could do
business.

Washington was a good choice for the young architect.
By the turn of the century enough time had passed since
slavery for a small but vigorous black middle class to
develop. Sidney was commissioned for a number of small
black projects, but chafed at the bit for a really big contract
in order to prove his talents. His opportunity came in 1907
when he was selected to prepare the plans for and superin-
tend the construction of a $75,000 building for the colored
branch of the Young Men's Christian Association on 12th
Street. It was with the commission earned from this job that
he had enough money to marry Portia and move her into a
new house.

In the first years of his marriage the big dreams that Sidney had written to Portia about seemed to be coming true.
He had won through competition the singular honor of

designing the Negro Building for the national tercentennial exposition at Jamestown, Virginia, in 1907. This $40,000 building was erected under his direction in only eighty days by an all-black construction crew. The following year Sidney was contracted by the District of Columbia as architect for the $90,000 Garfield Public School. Returning, probably with some sense of triumph, to Tuskegee, he completed plans and specifications for a new agricultural building, to cost $30,000. He went on to oversee the construction of two buildings at the black Kentucky Normal and Industrial Institute and the remodeling of a large hotel in Norfolk, Virginia.

Portia's new house had been designed and built by her husband in the new community of Fairmont Heights, Maryland. Sidney had organized and served as president of the Fairmont Heights Improvement Company. Through this investment company, the young architect and several black associates hoped to develop Fairmont Heights as a viable alternative to inner-city ghetto living. Sidney could not do enough, it seemed to his proud young wife. He was elected president of the Heights Citizens' Committee and of the Washington, D.C., chapter of the Negro Business League. The national league had been organized by his father-in-law in 1900 and Sidney sought now to further its work by editing its monthly magazine, the *Negro Business League Herald*.

At home, Portia was struggling to become a proper wife. She loved her beautiful new house, which years later she would still speak of with pride. When Booker gave her a piano as a belated wedding present, her surroundings were complete. She was grateful that her stepmother, Maggie, had forced her to learn housekeeping in spite of her resistance at the time. Settling down was difficult after the kind of independent life she had led. But she had her music and her husband seemed to love it almost as much as she did.

In the spring of her first year of marriage, Portia was again in that spotlight she so loved. She gave a classical concert in Washington for the benefit of a young black violinist, Clarence Cameron White. Portia was particularly enthusiastic about this concert because it raised funds to send White to Europe for further musical study.

But Portia was not to have much time to devote to her music. In that same year, 1908, her first child, a son, Sidney, Jr., was born. A second son was born October 3, 1909, and he was named Booker. Even though handicapped with the care of small children, Portia refused to be slowed down. Her father was often in Washington and she managed whenever possible to be included in his sphere of activity.

One time in particular she remembered because it involved the President of the United States. It was in 1908 and Booker had been invited to meet with Theodore Roosevelt at the White House. Portia convinced her father to allow her to accompany him. Sidney was only three months old and Portia could not find anyone to stay with him. Undaunted, Portia wrapped Sidney up and took him with her to the White House. President Roosevelt seemed to have been charmed and invited Portia to call again for tea.

What a contrast this visit was to Booker's first visit to the White House in October of 1901. By 1901 Booker was nationally recognized as the leading citizen of his race. Upon assuming the presidency after the assassination of McKinley in September 1901, Roosevelt immediately sought Booker's council on political appointments of both blacks and whites in the South. Roosevelt needed the black vote if he expected to be successful in the next election while also having high regard for Booker's *détente* with white conservatives whose support he also needed. To the Yankee aristocrat a dinner invitation to a respected adviser was nothing out of the ordinary. At eight that evening President and Mrs. Roosevelt, daughter Alice, three of the Roosevelt sons, and a close friend, Philip Stewart, all sat down to dinner with the black man. The reverberations from that simple act of social amenity were felt across the entire country. Roosevelt was condemned for socializing with a "nigger" and Booker, for presuming to step out of his class. The furor eventually died down but Booker was consigned to being a "silent" but still powerful adviser to that President except in official public circumstances. Thus Booker's 1908 White House visit was very formal and passed unnoted except in Portia's carefully tended store of memories of her father.

But then, Booker was no stranger to controversy. He seemed to take it easily in stride and to even thrive on it. Ten years later, in March of 1911, the New York *Times* reported Booker's arrest on charges of having assaulted a white woman in New York City. The charges were lodged by a white man named Ulrich who had attacked Booker upon observing him seemingly lurking in the vestibule of his home at 11½ West Sixty-third Street. Ulrich's wife was walking a dog in front of the house and, becoming frightened at seeing a black man, summoned her husband. The man set upon Booker with a stick, chasing and beating him all the way to nearby Central Park. The assailant was joined by another white man and Booker was knocked to the pavement nearly unconscious. A policeman interceded and hauled Ulrich and his victim to jail.

At the precinct house, Booker recovered sufficiently to identify himself and was immediately released. One account said that he went to Flower Hospital with scalp wounds and one ear nearly torn off. Ulrich was charged with assault and released on bail variously reported as amounting to $300,

William Sidney Pittman, c. 1910, during the early years of his marriage to Portia. *Schomburg Center, The New York Public Library, Astor, Lenox and Tilden Foundations*

Sidney Pittman, Jr., and his mother, Portia Washington Pittman, in 1946 at Harlem's famous Hotel Theresa where they stayed while in New York for the installation of Booker T. Washington as the first black man in the Hall of Fame. *Schomburg Center, The New York Public Library, Astor, Lenox and Tilden Foundations*

Sidney J. Phillips, in 1953, whose high-power drive for the Booker T. Washington Birthplace Memorial brought him into direct conflict with the fiery black congressman Adam Clayton Powell, Jr. *Schomburg Center, The New York Public Library Astor, Lenox and Tilden Foundations*

Left, Portia (*left*) and Fannie (*right*) at a rare family reunion in 1962 with Booker Pittman (*center*), Portia's prodigal son and the man credited with introducing jazz to South America. *Johnson Publishing Company*

Below, the reconstructed birthplace and childhood slave home of Booker T. Washington, realization of his daughter's greatest dream. The site was authorized as a U. S. National Monument in 1956.
National Park Service,
U. S. Department of the Interior

"... I have no real regrets.
I would rather be the poor daughter of
Booker T. Washington
than a rich daughter
of the wealthiest man on earth."
Portia in 1965. *Bob Burchette,*
Washington *Post*

Portia, then-Superintendent Fred A.
Wingeier and Associate Director A.
Clark Stratton at the dedication of the
Visitor Center of the Booker T.
Washington National Monument
in 1966. *National Park Service,*
U. S. Department of the Interior

$500, and $1,500. The local press followed the ensuing court hearing in detail but with a noticeable sympathy toward Booker. Booker made a public statement to the effect that he had been going to meet a Tuskegee employee at an address that had been supplied to him in a letter he had subsequently discarded. He had been checking the mail boxes for the name of the person he vaguely remembered that his friend was staying with when he was attacked by Ulrich. To quote Booker's exact statement to the press:

> I was not intoxicated; I had not touched a drop of liquor that night. I went to the house at No. 11½ West Sixty-third Street on a legitimate mission. I had never been there before. I destroyed the letter in which were the directions for me to go to that address in search of Daniel C. Smith, auditor of Tuskegee Institute. I did not speak to, recognize or approach any woman from the time I left my hotel until I was attacked in the vestibule of the house.
>
> I do not know what will be the effect of this affair on the work which I am doing for the emancipation of the negro [sic]. I have been embarrassed on my visits to New York by being saluted by handsomely gowned, attractive women while I have been walking in the streets. I could not remember whether I had met them in my work, although this may have been the case, so I did not respond to their salutations.

Support for Booker's innocence rained in from all quarters. His suite at the Hotel Manhattan was filled with flowers and telegrams, including one from President Taft reaffirming his confidence in the "leader of his race." Ulrich also received a small measure of support. A group of white citizens in Greenville, Alabama, started a subscription fund to pay for his defense.

But Booker was too powerful a man to be compromised long. The newspapers were even to publish a letter from the Children's Aid and Protection Society of Orange, N.J., stating that Ulrich was a wayward father of two, who had left his wife without support and was living in a common-law marriage with the woman who had started the entire affair.

The first day of the hearing, Booker arrived with a full contingent of influential supporters including the black former lieutenant governor of Louisiana, P. B. S. Pinchback. The case dragged on for some time, finally ending with a hung jury. It was never retried. Friends of Booker encouraged him to press assault charges against Ulrich, but Booker, perhaps out of a sense of *noblesse oblige*, refused and the case was quickly forgotten. Portia, however, fumed at the mere mention of the incident and was quick to point out that nothing was ever proven.

Life went on and Portia presented Booker with yet another grandchild in 1912. Her name was Fannie, with an "ie" to distinguish her from Portia's mother, and she was to become Booker's favorite. Portia remembered taking Fannie to see her grandfather in Oklahoma for a meeting of the National Negro Business League. Fannie started to sing to Booker, "It's a Long Way to Tipperary." Booker was enthralled because it was so perfectly pitched by the infant Fannie. Portia had tried to sing as a youngster, but Booker had expressed relief when she took up the piano instead.

In the meantime, Sidney Pittman was struggling to make ends meet for his growing family. The prominent architectural contracts had begun to dry up and with them, his prospects for status and financial security. It is not exactly clear what brought about Sidney's failing fortunes. He had always been a difficult man to get along with, with a temper that quickly flared when he thought his dignity had been affronted. As Booker T. Washington's son-in-law he was no doubt favored in the awarding of architectural contracts for black projects. This fact perhaps began to grate on his self-esteem and contributed to the increasing moodiness which made it harder and harder for him to find work. He had seen his grand scheme for a black owned and operated theater and office building in downtown Washington go down the drain with the collapse of the Lincoln Memorial Building Company which he had founded. Fairmont Heights resisted the major growth he had envisaged. And now he saw his wife having to give private piano lessons to supplement their income.

Sidney was a proud man, who refused to accept the limitations imposed on him by his color. He probably looked with some jealousy at his father-in-law who openly consorted with white millionaires and Presidents. Sidney had made such big promises while winning his wife, and as his prospects spiraled downward he was filled with bitterness that he could not make them come true. He had not always been hostile to Booker. Portia remembered them often sitting on the porch out in Fairmont Heights, laughing and eating southern food together. But Sidney began to seek elsewhere for fulfillment, and in 1913 he moved his family to Dallas, Texas, away from the city dominated by his father-in-law's presence.

He had secured a commission to design the Dallas Pythian Temple for the Knights of Pythias, a Masonic organization. He oversaw its complete construction, which was of such excellence that it stands today as the home of the Dallas Union Bankers Life Insurance Company. But this success was not accomplished without obstacle. Sidney was a very exacting man. While he was a strong race man and tried to hire blacks whenever possible, he demanded that his workmen perform as well as, if not better than, their white counterparts. His strict attitude hardly endeared him to his employees or, for that matter, to his employers.

Portia remembered that one of these workmen tried to kill her husband. Sidney was on a high scaffold overseeing the work on the temple when one of the construction crew approached him and an argument ensued. Sidney was knocked down and was about to be pushed over the side to a long drop below when another workman intervened and saved his life. Portia remembered the rescuer's name as being Armstrong. Unlike his fellow workmen, Armstrong had developed a regard for Sidney which after this incident would protect him throughout the rest of the construction of the temple.

In Dallas, Sidney moved his family into a home at 2213 Juliette Street and Portia resumed giving private piano lessons. She saw little of her father since his fund-raising activities after 1905 had been concentrated in and around New York City. However, they resumed their lively correspondence of earlier years, and Portia followed his every move as reported in the press. The latter was not difficult as one of the things that made Booker so formidable was the constant stream of publicity given him by both the black and white press. While it was true that the race leader made good copy, his detractors felt the publicity was more the result of the releases and articles with which the Institute bombarded the press. Articles constantly appeared in print under Booker's name and by 1912 he had published some thirteen books. Booker was a man of action, so by necessity much of his work was ghost written, including his famous autobiography, *Up from Slavery*. Max Bennett Thrasher, a New England journalist and teacher, was the fortunate choice for this international best seller. Emmett Scott, Washington's trusted secretary, was also to do a large share of his employer's writing.

Booker was indeed a man of action who by his mid-fifties was still maintaining the grueling pace of his younger days. Members of Tuskegee's board of trustees saw the toll being taken on his health and arranged for him to return to Europe in 1910. Rather than rest, Booker roamed the Continent for three months studying the conditions of the working classes. He was in constant demand as a speaker who brought good tidings of great progress in the United States. An open message to the people of Europe repudiating Booker's contention was issued by a distinguished group of black professionals, clergymen, and editors:

> Against this dominant tendency [oppression at home] strong and brave Americans, White and Black, are fighting, but they need, and need badly, the moral support of England and Europe in their crusade for the recognition of manhood . . . It is a blow in the face to have one, who himself suffers daily insult and humiliation in America, give the impression that all is well.

The signers of this statement included W. E. B. Du Bois, William Monroe Trotter, Bishop Alexander Walters, J. Max Barber, Archibald Grimké, and N. F. Mossell, a physican and uncle to Paul Robeson, the singer, who was to make a similar appeal fifty years later.

But Booker T. Washington was lionized on both sides of the Atlantic and, unlike his critics, he had the ear of the wealthiest people in both places. He prevailed upon Julius Rosenwald, president of Sears, Roebuck and Company, to establish 4,500 rural school houses throughout the South for black youth. As late as 1914 he was pressing Andrew Carnegie to underwrite the construction and operations of a "Tuskegee" in Liberia, West Africa. Former President Theodore Roosevelt became a member of the Tuskegee board of trustees. Between 1910 and 1913 six major buildings were erected on the campus, including the John A. Andrew Memorial Hospital. The following year Booker succeeded in launching National Negro Health Week.

By this time, Booker's failing health was easily observable. No amount of admonishing from friends or doctors would get him to slow down. He traveled constantly and, even when home, refused to succumb to his encroaching weakness. Against the counsel of his physician in August of 1915 he traveled to Boston to speak before the National Negro Business League. A few days later he was speaking in Chicago. His last official appearance occurred October 25 when he spoke before the National Council of Congregational Churches in New Haven, Connecticut.

Shortly thereafter Booker T. Washington was hospitalized in New York at the Rockefeller Institute. The medical report indicated that "not a single organ of his body is functioning more than five percent of normal." He remained at Rockefeller for several weeks and was then transferred to St. Luke's Hospital where it was hoped that his condition would improve. Sensing that death was imminent, Booker insisted on being taken home. He was accompanied to Tuskegee by his personal physician, Dr. John A. Kenny, who sent back to Booker's anxious friends in New York the following telegram:

NOVEMBER 14, 1915
REACHED HERE WITH PATIENT AT HALF-PAST TWELVE THIS
MORNING. END CAME AT FIFTEEN MINUTES OF FIVE.

Portia, in Dallas, was giving a lesson on the Steinway that had been the wedding gift from her father when she was told of his death. Now indeed a "fatherless child," she would mourn her father's death the rest of her life with a bitter sense that he would have lived so much longer had he not worked so hard in building a viable black institution in white America against the constant opposition of his critics, black and white.

Booker's funeral occasioned a national and international outpouring of sympathy. Nora Holt, the black music critic for the *Chicago Defender* and the *New York Age,* remembered the obituary that appeared in the Hong Kong newspaper while she was there. It went to great lengths to extoll his virtue as a great teacher and man, never singling out the fact that he was black.

America and the black race had lost a truly great leader. Even one of his staunchest critics, W. E. B. Du Bois acknowledged that a certain debt of gratitude was owed to Booker T. Washington. Not again until Martin Luther King, Jr., with the possible limited exception of Marcus Garvey, were we to see a black leader of his magnitude and power.

Even in death, Booker was to put his public obligation ahead of his family. Maggie was designated executor of his will because he knew she would continue as firm in her commitment to Tuskegee as he would have been. Portia and her brothers were willed The Oaks and all of its furnishings. There was great criticism of this by people who felt that the house and its contents should remain in the control of Tuskegee as a shrine to Booker. The house remained intact and was occupied by Maggie until her death.

After the funeral, Portia returned to Dallas and resumed her role as mother and wife. The family had moved into a house on Germania Street the previous year and Portia was still trying to make it livable. In an interview some years later, she was to acknowledge how handy the sewing training she hated at Tuskegee turned out to be for her during the lean years of her early married life.

Sidney was still struggling to establish himself. He had completed work on the St. James. A.M.E. Church, but few whites sought the services of this first black Dallas architect.

There were a few other church commissions, but blacks who could afford his service usually took their business to whites. This kind of reverse racism on the part of his own people enraged Sidney. He became a trial to live with and increasingly more bitter.

Just as in Washington, D.C., much of Sidney's lack of acceptance was largely of his own making. He was highly individualistic and an eccentric in a time and place that were intolerant of such behavior, especially in a black man. Over the years he had come to wear his hair slightly long and he always looked as if he had slept in his suit. Portia recalled that he wore the same clothes over and over, his mind being on other than material things. He was extremely moody (a trait his daughter, Fannie, was to manifest also) and would awaken in the night to brood over his problems. In addition to his appearance and personality, Sidney's problems stemmed from the fact that professionally he was very exacting and severe in his standards. For this he gained a few small jobs and some measure of respect from the white Dallas community. But members of the black community found him arrogant and considered him too big for his breeches. Sidney, in return, felt that his fine training and experience were unappreciated. After all, the design of the Negro Building at the Jamestown exposition in 1907 made him the first black to be awarded a contract by the federal government.

There was a fire in the house on Germania Street around 1918 in which the biggest loss was all of Portia's books, but Sidney's earnings were still sufficient then to move his family without delay into another house at 1018 Liberty. Sidney continued for a few more years thereafter to try to work within the established order, becoming in 1925, the president of the Brotherhood of Negro Building Mechanics of Texas. That same year the *Dallas City Directory* listed, in addition to Sidney, Portia as "teacher Booker. T. Washington H.S."

It is not clear whether Portia undertook a full-time teaching job because of the family's finances or because of her desire for personal fulfillment. It was probably a combination of the two. The Pittman children were growing up and becoming increasingly more self-sufficient.

Fannie and Booker had both begun to display a flair for music. They also shared a devilish streak that kept the truant officer calling at the Pittman home. In contrast, Sidney, Jr., was a scholar, who graduated at the head of his Dallas high school class in June 1925.

That same month Portia's stepmother died. Maggie had remained active in Tuskegee affairs up until a month before her death. After Booker's death, she had made numerous speeches before women's clubs in the South and the East. In 1923, as president of the Women's Colored Clubs, she had addressed the annual meeting of the Women's Auxiliary of the East Alabama Presbytery at Montgomery, Alabama. This was the first appearance of a black person before a white audience in the history of Montgomery, the cradle of the Confederacy.

Maggie spent her final days at The Oaks, dying quietly in her sleep June 4, 1925. She had lived long enough after her husband to see him immortalized in an inspiring statue raised at Tuskegee through the contribution of $25,000 from blacks throughout the country. Of the funds collected there is record of $525.31 coming from Dallas, probably raised through Portia's efforts.

Booker T. Washington was a revered hero in Dallas. The high school that all Portia's children eventually attended was named for him, and around 1924 Portia was personally invited by the principal, Joseph J. Rhoads, to teach music there. She undertook this job even though she had a full load of private piano students and was directing two choral clubs and the local church choir. She was also chairman of the education department of the Texas Association of Negro Musicians.

Portia taught successfully for a year at the high school, but in her second year she was challenged on her credentials. It was at this time that Portia was to begin a correspondence with her old New England contacts that was to prevail into her latest years.

The Texas state education laws had become more stringent after she started teaching, requiring that teachers be fully certified in order to work in the public schools. Portia wrote to the Bradford Academy in Massachusetts, requesting the administration there to contact the superintendent of the Texas State Department of Education, Mr. S. M. N. Marrs, on her behalf. Miss Pond, the assistant principal of Bradford, responded immediately to Portia's request. She remembered Portia as a brilliant music student when she was still a teacher at Bradford.

Miss Pond wrote to Marrs about Bradford's high level of scholarship which made Portia's junior and senior years there equivalent to the first two years of a state university. She pointed out Portia's years of musical training abroad and the work she had done since as a teacher of piano and chorus. "We are not making a special plea," she wrote, "on the ground that Mrs. Pittman is the daughter of Dr. Booker Washington, for we feel sure that he believed that merit should stand on its own feet."

Miss Pond pressed the case further by having a new librarian at Bradford, Ermine Stone, write to a friend in Texas who was a niece of the superintendent. Miss Stone, was a graduate of the University of Texas and Miss Pond had been quick to pick up on Portia's inference in her letters that there was either a prejudice against or lack of knowledge about eastern schools down there in Texas.

It was truly an unhappy time for Portia. Not since that desolate year at Wellesley had she had to prove her worth and her superiority. By November 1925 she was still being paid half salary for her work as director of the choir at the high school. Her letters to Bradford were full of longing for the good old student days. She expressed a desire to bring her Aida Choral Club to Bradford and, when no paid invitation was forthcoming, she settled for inviting Miss Pond to listen to the radio broadcast that they were to do soon on the Dallas news station.

Portia was to receive another setback when she expressed to Miss Pond the desire to send her daughter, Fannie, to Bradford after she finished high school in Dallas. Miss Pond, kindly, liberal, but Yankee pragmatic, wrote the following to Portia:

November 11, 1925

You speak of hoping to send your Fannie here in two years. I wish I could see you to talk with you about this face to face. I know that you now look back to Bradford days as happy ones, but is not that partly because the years have dimmed much that was very hard? Difficulties that you would hesitate to put upon a child of your own? I wish I could say that the North had less prejudice than twenty years ago, but I cannot. Things happen right here in Massachusetts which make my blood boil because of the cruelty of the prejudice. On the other hand, are there not more opportunities for Colored girls in the larger colleges and state universities than ever before? If she can get the High School fitting for a state University, will she not be freer from the cruel limitations of the smaller schools? I, personally, have not changed, Portia, only to the extent that I just cannot

93

bear to have a young girl put in such a hard place, far from home. I hope I have not hurt you by writing so frankly, and I trust you understand my motive.

Fannie was thirteen years old and had already begun to display a talent for singing and the piano. Her interest tended toward the blues and jazz, in which she was strongly influenced by her brother Booker, who was equally talented on the clarinet and saxophone.

Booker had learned the rudiments of music from his mother, as had a number of Dallas boys such as Dan Minor, Sammy Price, and Budd Johnson, who were all to become professional musicians. In high school, Booker, Budd, and Dan pulled their friends together into a group that they named the "Blue Moon Chasers." The group stayed intact for three years, playing at picnics, school dances, and even an occasional out-of-town function in the Dallas vicinity. In 1927 Booker joined up with Jesse Stone's Blues Serenaders, which gave him a chance to make his first phonograph recording, on the Okeh label.

Portia did not care much at first for her son's brand of music, but she was very proud of his talent and encouraged him. Sidney, Jr., had gone on to Howard University in Washington, D.C., with an interest in his father's field, architecture. Portia wanted him to go to an eastern school but at Howard, a federally funded black school, he was able to get financial aid and to work part time to support himself.

Money was short in the Pittman household and the atmosphere increasingly more tense. Sidney continued to rail against the forces that he believed were trying to keep him down. Chief on his list were the leaders of the black community. He had already quarreled with the Knights of Pythias, believing that they had not paid him enough for his work. Sidney placed great value on his skills and was embittered when he saw the few blacks with money turning to

white architects, many of whom he considered inferior workmen. And in 1927 even his wife was to further wound his
largish ego and plunge him into deeper remorse when she
gained a brief prominence that she was to remember as one
of the high points of her life.

The National Education Association (NEA) held its annual convention in Dallas in March of 1927. Over seventy-
five hundred educators poured into the city. Whether because of the fear of "Jim Crow" laws and mistreatment or
because of the long distance to Dallas, few of the fifty black
educators usually active with the NEA attended. The two or
three who did were either Texans or ex-Texans. It was ironic
considering that the most memorable part of the convention
was black—the performance by a six-hundred-voice Booker
T. Washington High School chorus under the direction of
Mrs. Portia Washington Pittman.

The training of the chorus had consumed three solid
months of Portia's time. A great deal was riding on the success of its performance. It was the first time in the history of
the NEA that a group of black high school students was to
appear on its convention program. According to the Dallas
Express (February 26, 1927), "This important undertaking
is a matter of grave concern to the entire Dallas citizenship,
white and black alike."

Portia was under tremendous pressure but, secretly, she
was thrilled by the challenge. She would be back in the
spotlight, and *she* would show them. All those people who
belittled or just plain disbelieved what she had told about
her background would get their comeuppance. She also felt
she would be following in her father's footsteps by demon-
strating clearly that black people could excel when given
opportunity and properly prepared.

The night of the performance, the auditorium at the fair
grounds was filled to capacity with conventioneers. (The

Dallas citizenry, black and white, would have to wait until the following week when a repeat performance was scheduled in larger quarters at City Hall.) The crowd was not disappointed. The Dallas newspapers raved over the chorus, briefly uniting the black and white communities in civic pride. From the Dallas *Express* (March 5, 1927):

600 VOICE HI SCHOOL CHORUS CHARMS
N.E.A. CONVENTION.
CONVENTION HALL PACKED AS STUDENT
CHORUS OF 600 FROM BOOKER WASHINGTON
HIGH SCHOOL, DIRECTED BY DAUGHTER
OF ILLUSTRIOUS EDUCATOR, GIVES THIRTY-
MINUTE PROGRAM OF SPIRITUALS . . .

Not only did roar upon roar of applause from 7,500 pairs of hands greet every number rendered by the 600-voice mass chorus of The Booker Washington High School when it appeared before the National Education Association in the Auditorium of the Fair Grounds on last Tuesday evening, but President Randall J. Condon, Master of Ceremonies for the evening, went into the wings as the program closed and Mrs. Portia Washington Pittman, conductress, left the stage, urged her to return and requested that she lead the whole assembly in singing the old familiar tunes of "Swanee River," "Old Black Joe" and "Carry Me Back to Old Virginia." And never before in the history of the association has there been such harmony produced to the rhythm as beat by the baton of this conductress. They all sang with the chorus; then sat again in utter silence until the last golden echoes of "Couldn't Hear Nobody Pray" had died away, burst again into applause as the students began to move from the stage, and members of the official family rushed to the wings to meet and congratulate Mrs. Pittman. . . . Said Principal Peterson, member of the Executive Committee and head of one of the largest High Schools of Los Angeles, ". . . I have never in my life been so affected by the evident soul of music as I have been here with this chorus. And you can never know just how much this chorus has done to encourage real study of the needs of the Negro. The impression will be a lasting one."

. . . It was a complete success from the moment that Mrs. Pittman was introduced as the daughter of Booker T. Washington, until the last student had left his place on the stage.

Years later, Portia would still flush with pride and happiness in telling of her triumph: "White people in the South had never heard Negro spirituals sung like the way I taught them. Because I had a German training that gave me the artistic part and I added things. For instance, there was a song called 'O Mary Don't You Weep, Don't You Moan.' White people had never heard the song before and they put it in the school text book the following year as a new beautiful Negro spiritual."

Her triumph now a part of history, Portia returned to the realities of life. She resumed teaching and, giving piano lessons on the side, struggled to keep the family together; but one by one the ties that bound them were breaking. Sidney, Jr., was gone and Fannie was near to graduating from junior high school. Booker had joined a small combo led by the yet little known Count Basie and was playing at the Subway Club in Kansas City. His growing reputation as an outstanding saxophonist was soon to take him east with a band headed by Blanche Calloway (Cab Calloway's sister) and into a larger world from which he would never return home.

In the summer of 1927 Portia sent Fannie to camp outside of Dallas and sought relief for herself from her frustrations

97

and problems by enrolling in a six-week vocal music course at Columbia University in New York City. Portia had many fond memories of New York. Her father had spent a great deal of time there doing business and the Washington family had summered on Long Island. Portia looked up her father's old acquaintances and enjoyed the comfort of being with people who knew and esteemed what she liked to call her "heritage."

By the time of Portia's return to New York the Harlem Renaissance was in full flower. The once upper-middle-class white area of Harlem was now solidly black and had become a lodestone for the most talented young blacks of post-World War I America. W. E. B. Du Bois gave voice to the political and economic demands of a new generation of blacks through his dynamic editorship of *The Crisis* magazine, published by the National Association for the Advancement of Colored People. The NAACP had grown, from its birth as a protest against Booker T. Washington, into a national organization dedicated to securing full citizenship for blacks in America. Booker attempted to thwart its development, but with his death the NAACP quickly moved to assume the leadership role he had played. However, it launched a program of action that attacked the very foundations of the Washington philosphy. Basic to its policy was the repudiation of any accommodation to white racist institutions.

In more contemporary times the black activist Rap Brown would say that "violence is as American as Cherry Pie." Violence to the Negro reached epidemic proportions in the closing years of the nineteenth century. More than twenty-five hundred blacks were lynched between 1884 and 1900. The pattern continued during the Booker Washington years, but it remained for a more progressive, northern group of spokesmen to bring it to light as a national scandal.

Booker had not been immune to the terrorism against his people and in private communication had written of his anguish. But his was the way of accommodation, which meant to him that even this violence would work itself out.

By the time of his death, the Ku Klux Klan had revived to declare war on all blacks, Jews, Roman Catholics, and persons of foreign birth. Hooded night riders were seen on the streets of rural towns from New England to Texas. Fear, crop failures, and the lure of jobs in World War I industries sent waves of black immigrants north to form the ghettos that exploded in riots, two of the worst occurring in East St. Louis, Illinois, in 1915, and Chicago in 1919. Many of the 367,000 black soldiers, who served in the armed forces returned from World War I demanding a fair share of the democracy for which they fought and died. But within the first year after the end of the war ten black soldiers, several still wearing their uniforms, were lynched in the South.

The NAACP took the lead in gathering statistics about lynchings and publishing them with full accounts of the events leading up to the lynchings. In 1917 Du Bois and James Weldon Johnson, secretary of the NAACP, organized a protest parade of blacks who marched down Fifth Avenue in New York completely silent except for the muffled sound of drums. They carried signs that read, MOTHER, DO LYNCHERS GO TO HEAVEN? and MR. PRESIDENT, WHY NOT MAKE AMERICA SAFE FOR DEMOCRACY?

But postwar Harlem had another side which was more in keeping with Portia's nature. The Harlem Renaissance was primarily a cultural movement that saw the emergence of such talented writers as Langston Hughes, Jean Toomer, Zora Neale Hurston, Claude McKay, and Countee Cullen. Jessie Richmond Fauset, beginning with her 1924 novel *There Is Confusion*, introduced a new genre of black literature. Black theater, practically dormant since 1910, played to capacity crowds impressed by the talents of such performers as Paul Robeson, Rose McClendon, and Charles Gilpin. Abbie Mitchell, Portia's friend from her Berlin days, was a popular concert artist, who had been drawn back by the Renaissance to the city in which she grew up. In musical theater, F. E. Miller, Aubrey Lyles, Noble Sissle, and Eubie Blake wrote and produced in 1921 the smash revue, *Shuffle Along.* This show, which included the hit songs "I'm Just Wild About Harry" and "Love Will Find a Way," was the first in a succession of black musicals which introduced over the decade such talents as Ethel Waters and Josephine Baker.

The leading hostess of the period was A'Lelia Walker, the daughter of Madam C. J. Walker, the first businesswoman in America black or white to make a million dollars. The Walker fortune was built on a hair-straightening preparation invented by Madam Walker and parlayed into a network of highly profitable beauty shops and schools across the country. Booker T. Washington had frequently been a guest in her elegant Harlem townhouse and Tuskegee was the recipient of over twelve thousand dollars before her death in 1919. A'Lelia continued the grand life style of large touring cars, imported furnishings, and a country estate bequeathed her by her mother. Though brief, Portia's contact with such elegance and the excitement of Harlem renewed her spirit.

Portia returned to Dallas confident that her college level course work would confirm her credentials for teaching in the Texas school system. But coming home to her husband was another matter. Sidney vacillated now between moody states of depression over his floundering career and violent fits of rage at the hypocrisy of the black community which he thought set his fellow blacks against him. Architectural contracts were few and far between; thus Portia, through teaching and piano lessons, had to become the financial mainstay of the family. While she understood the artistic nature of men like her husband ("You just have to be clinging and helpless, letting them think that they are the big cheese"), she grew to resent his jealousy of her moderate achievements and the schism he caused with their children. Fannie had dropped out of high school and was moldering in the backwash of Dallas' limited black cultural life. Booker was long gone, refusing to be hemmed in by his father's strictness. And Sidney, Jr., was still struggling alone in Washington to educate himself, with little financial help from home.

Rather than be destroyed, Portia began to seek alternatives to her dilemma. She wrote to her father's successor at Tuskegee, Dr. Robert R. Moton, about coming there to teach. Moton had been a loyal admirer of her father's and he was to express great concern for his predecessor's daughter.

Portia did not really want to leave her husband but there came one night in 1928 when Sidney provoked a particularly violent argument with his daughter. Fannie had inherited her father's volatile temper and would press him as far as he pressed her. In the heat of their disagreement, Sidney struck his daughter hard across the face. Fannie crumpled before the blow and was sick for several days afterward.

Fannie recovered but Portia felt that this trauma was the cause of the epileptic seizures that her daughter was to be periodically subject to for the rest of her life. Sidney was repentant, but his abuse of Fannie was the final act for which his wife could not forgive him. Portia packed up Fannie and went home to Tuskegee.

Portia's return to her birthplace in 1928 was not exactly

ignominious and old friends of her father tried to make her welcome. Dr. Moton arranged quarters for them in the dormitory and gave Portia a position on the faculty. Mother and daughter settled into the Tuskegee community with little trouble and by 1931 the summer school bulletin could list Portia as teaching "Music 30—Public School Music— Glee Club and Choral Singing." Any thoughts of returning to Dallas were deterred by Sidney's continuing state of rage against his fellow blacks. By 1931 his outspoken criticism had taken on a new dimension with his launching of a weekly newspaper, *Brotherhood Eyes*.

As editor and publisher, Sidney had a public platform from which he could carry on his campaign against what he saw as the hypocrisy of certain members of the black community in Dallas. His main targets were black ministers. He excoriated them for publicly preaching the Gospel and taking their parishioners' money, while leading private lives characterized by less than moral rectitude. He took on other segments of the black establishment, accusing them of racial hypocrisy. Using his own experience but citing others as well, he reported on the employment of whites over qualified blacks for certain ventures by blacks who publicly proclaimed their commitment to civil rights.

No copies of *Brotherhood Eyes* seem to have survived, but Portia remembered them being as brilliantly written as they were scandalous. The uproar that Sidney created was so great in black Dallas that even today an elderly member of the Knights of Pythias became very upset, refusing to discuss the matter at all with the author. Somehow Sidney himself survived, even to being acquitted of libel by the Dallas courts in 1936. It was probably because there was sufficient truth in his accusations and the white community so thoroughly enjoyed his exposés that he was able to continue.

In retrospect, Portia enjoyed telling of the hell her husband raised. But at the time it created great hardship for her and the children. She felt that had her husband been more like her father, he could have risen above the challenges to his integrity and gone about doing what he thought to be right. But Sidney had brought his burden home and taken it out on his family. There was no going back, and by spring of 1932 Portia was having her own problems at Tuskegee, which could be characterized as professional *déjà vu.*

Tuskegee had undergone great change since Booker Washington's day. The 1920s had seen the emergence of the "New Negro" which resulted in a flowering of black intellectual and artistic accomplishment that rendered the concept of consigning blacks to industrial training obsolete. In addition, the institution of the first modern income tax law in 1913 had imposed restraints on white philanthropy with which Booker for the most part had not had to contend. In order to be able to compete with other black institutions, and their liberal arts thrust, for the now limited philanthropic dollar, Tuskegee, under Dr. Moton, expanded its academic departments and upgraded vocational education to a college level. This change was also a pragmatic response to the rising level of education throughout the country which limited the job market potential of the traditional Tuskegee graduate. The first junior college diploma was awarded in 1927 and the first bachelor's degree in 1928. Three years later, the School of Music was formally established under the direction of a brilliant musician and composer, William L. Dawson.

Portia had great respect for Dawson's talents, but his exacting academic requirements for members of his staff sent

Portia back to corresponding with her old New England contacts:

April 2, 1932

My dear Miss Pond:

For the last three years I have been at this school, serving as choir director and teacher of piano.

The school of music now has a new director for this year who is a "degree fiend." Your training and experience amount to very little with him, and it is quite embarrassing to have preference given to young girls just out of school with no experience . . .

I am again asking you to send any "B.A." credits together with a [sic] "05" catalogue.

Perhaps you knew that my dear Prof. Downes gave all of my lessons to me free of charge. I would appreciate a letter from you mentioning this and also telling of my music at Bradford. You were so lovely to help me get the Texas certificate . . .

I believe it possible to do anything you make up your mind to do. I feel as young and vigorous as I did twenty-five years ago . . .

I do hope you are well and happy as you deserve to be. I am hoping someday to visit my old haunts—especially Bradford . . .

Much love to you and please remember me to other friends.

From Portia

Portia received an immediate response from Miss Pond at Bradford, which had been renamed, in 1932, Bradford Junior College. She had met with the Bradford registrar and together they put together a record that demonstrated Portia's successful matriculation in college-level courses her last two years at Bradford. "After all, the music is the thing," Miss

Pond wrote, "that should count most toward a degree . . . and that you can demonstrate . . . don't be discouraged by college registrars. I was years and years between periods of study in getting my A.B. from the University of Michigan in 1916. It more than paid, for I did not have to keep explaining that experience is as good as those two little letters."

Never one to long indulge herself in self-pity, Portia began to think about returning to college and getting a degree. Columbia was appealing because she had enjoyed her summer course there in 1927 and she would be near Fannie and Booker. Fannie was enrolled in the Institute of Musical Arts (now the Juilliard School) in New York during the 1932–33 academic year. She majored in piano with Martinus Sieveking, and her course included theory, ear training, and keyboard studies.

Booker had left Kansas City to tour the mid-Atlantic and New England states with the Blanche Calloway band for a year. He was now based in New York as lead alto saxophonist with Ralph Cooper's Congo Knights. Booker's musical reputation was now solidly established and any band that picked him up seemed to enjoy long and successful engagements at such popular places as the Apollo Theater and the Harlem Opera House. He was briefly married during that period, but because the girl was white, Portia, still her father's child, was not sorry to see their relationship soon dissolved.

New York never materialized for Portia. In June of 1932 Booker sailed for Paris with the Lucky Millender band and Fannie transferred the following year to a conservatory in Detroit. Sidney, Jr., had been graduated from Howard University and was working in the Washington, D.C., Post Office. It was the bottom of the Depression and the Post Office offered, and would continue to offer for a long time, about the best job blacks could get. In fact, there have been more black holders of bachelor degrees and Ph.D.s that have worked in the U. S. Post Office than in any other American institution. Even though college trained, hard physical work was not new to Sidney, Jr. He had gotten through school by working in a restaurant opposite the old Howard Theater.

Portia helped him from her earnings after she left her husband and felt that she owed the same now to Fannie. The disagreement over her academic credentials was resolved and Portia continued on the Tuskegee music school staff. However, the Institute catalog for 1933–34 lists her only as teaching piano. The public school music and vocal courses had been taken over by degree holders. Dawson had gotten his way and appointed to his department only college graduates. But Portia was still to have the last laugh. Two of the most illustrious Dawson appointees were old friends of Portia's who had both spent time in Berlin—Abbie Mitchell and Hazel Harrison.

Abbie was head of the Vocal Department but found the South backward and repressive and relinquished her position in short order. Hazel, from Laporte, Indiana, was more amenable to sleepy Tuskegee than the northern born Abbie.

She had preceded Portia to Berlin, where she became a pupil of Victor Heinz and Ferruccio Busoni. The Germans had made constant comparison between the two "colored American pianists." Portia was flattered by the comparison because she truly liked and admired Hazel. After all, Hazel had made her debut with the Berlin Philharmonic Orchestra and would eventually go on to academic prominence at Howard University.

Portia was to live to speak of their long friendship at a memorial service for Hazel; but that was well into the future. For now, she was glad for the company of people who understood the fine training she had received. Portia felt generally unappreciated at Tuskegee. As much to annoy her

Portia in April 1970, at age eighty-seven, at the White House as the luncheon guest of Special Assistant to the President Robert J. Brown. *The White House, Courtesy of the New York* Amsterdam News

Portia Washington Pittman in 1971, at age eighty-eight, holding a photograph of herself from younger, better days. *Ruth Ann Stewart*

Portia entertaining during a visit to Bradford College in 1974. *Bradford College*

Portia Washington Pittman, at age ninety-one, in Washington, D.C., at the 1974 Emancipation Day celebration at Federal City College. *Washington* Post

colleagues as to revive old times, she would walk across the campus conversing with Hazel in German!

By 1939 Portia's name no longer appeared on the faculty roster. She built herself a small house off campus in which she opened a private music studio. She and Fannie shared the teaching load which had grown from twelve pupils to fifty-seven by the time the school was officially renamed the Booker T. Washington School of Music three years later.

Fannie, who had been living in Detroit, was on her way to a successful music career when she ran out of money and out of steam. In 1933–34, her first year at the Detroit conservatory, she won a medal for excellence, but jazz and blues were her first loves. Even her classical music teacher would let her interrupt their classical lessons together with a jazz piece. He was fascinated with the deep chords and, for him, the exotic melodies produced by Fannie's long fingers ranging back and forth over the keyboard. Fannie's musical ability seems to have been fairly good if we are to judge by the fact that at various times she shared the band stand with Count Basie, Louis Armstrong, and Bob Cuizzet. But recurring bouts of epilepsy and low finances combined to bring her back to Tuskegee in the late 1930s.

Portia was glad to have at least this one child home. Booker left Europe for South America in 1936 where he was to remain the next twenty-five years. Sidney, Jr., was to spend that much time and then some in Washington still working in the post office. Portia's brother Ernest Davidson Washington would die in 1942, without having contributed much to the Washington family image except for collecting and publishing his father's speeches ten years earlier. Her other brother, Booker Washington, Jr., was still alive but in ill health. He had been more successful, having owned and operated a real estate business and been a member of the school board in Los Angeles. By the early 1940s his son,

Booker Washington III, was working on a master's degree in architecture at New York University.

As for Sidney Pittman, Portia did not have much contact with him after she had left Dallas in 1928. She felt that he did not want a divorce but after the incident with Fannie, Portia would not even consider reconciliation. She did not completely forsake him and in her mind believed she saved him from a prison term.

Sidney continued to publish *Brotherhood Eyes* and in 1936 was taken to court for libel. According to the records of the Dallas County Courthouse, the charge of libel was dismissed upon written motion of the district attorney. Portia maintained, however, that Sidney's newspaper did eventually get him in trouble and he was sent to Leavenworth federal penitentiary, even though the authorities there can find no record for him under that name.

But Portia insisted that he spent one year of a five-year sentence there, enjoyably, as the prison librarian. He was supposedly released early because of the intercession of President Franklin D. Roosevelt. Portia said she brought this pardon about through her friendship with a Miss McDuffy who she identified as being Roosevelt's housekeeper. At Portia's request, Miss McDuffy approached the President who then looked into the matter and secured Pittman's release.

A search of contemporary Dallas newspapers turns up nothing about such a case, but there is one fact that emerges in support of Portia's story. There is no listing for Sidney in the *Dallas City Directory* between the years of 1937 and 1946, even though he was listed every other year, from his arrival in 1913 until two years before his death in 1958. What happened to William Sidney Pittman during those years is a mystery. Portia said that he did little as an architect after her departure in 1928 and from that year on he was never again listed as an architect in the *Dallas Directory*.

Portia's termination of any official connection with Tuskegee Institute was inevitable by the late 1930s. The Depression, which had swept away most signs of the prosperity of the previous decade, affected blacks especially hard. Tuskegee, as designed by its founder, was almost totally self-sufficient and faired better than other black schools. But fund raising had been more and more of an uphill battle which, along with several personal tragedies, took its toll on the health of the Institute's president, Robert Moton, forcing his retirement in 1935. With his departure, one of Portia's last links with her father was severed.

Robert Russa Moton had succeeded Booker T. Washington in 1915 as Tuskegee president at the express wish of the founder. Moton had been educated at Hampton Institute where he was serving as commandant of cadets, the only black to head a department there, when summoned to Tuskegee. Thoroughly steeped in the Hampton vocational tradition which had shaped Booker's thinking, Moton at first made no essential changes in the basic outlook and direction of Tuskegee. By the mid-1920s, however, he moved to upgrade the academic program to college and degree levels in response to the changing times. Even with this change, Moton was still charged by his critics with conducting an "Uncle Tom" institution. While he never wielded the massive power of Booker T. Washington, Moton continued to be consulted by important whites as spokesman for the black race, a practice which helped fan the flames of the Booker Washington controversy. Rather than abating with Booker's death, the vocational versus academic education of black men and women debate churned on. Even within the tight world of the Tuskegee campus the topic was explosive. Teachers had been dismissed for suggesting to some brighter students that they transfer to a higher-level institution.

After Moton's retirement in 1935, Portia found herself increasingly put into a position of defending her father. As the founder's daughter, she enjoyed a certain measure of respect, but less than she thought she deserved, given her father's great sacrifice for the school. With Moton, Portia could depend on support for both Booker's philosophy and her unique position as his daughter. But with the new president, Dr. Frederick D. Patterson, there was no such security. Born in 1901 in Washington, D.C., Patterson was educated in the North and rose through the Tuskegee ranks as an instructor of veterinary science to become president at the age of thirty-four. Catherine Moton, his predecessor's daughter, became his wife that same year after she graduated from the Conservatory of Music at Oberlin College. Even though Patterson respected Tuskegee's history and tradition, his administration was to bring changes in which Portia had no place. But before taking leave of her official Tuskegee duties, she was able to taste something of the pleasures of academic life and, as always, music was the center of her interest.

She gave unstintingly of her time to her students, one of the most outstanding being the author Ralph Ellison. Ellison was a music major, but in Portia's estimation he turned out to be a better writer (his critically acclaimed *The Invisible Man* was published in 1954) than he would have been a musician. There were other students she recalled, like Albert Murray who would remember her in his book *South to a Very Old Place*.

Through the years while Portia was a member of the faculty many black concert artists would visit the campus under an entertainment program inaugurated by President Moton—southern reality necessitated Tuskegee being self-sufficient even in matters of culture. Roland Hayes and Marian Anderson both lifted their magnificent voices in the Tuskegee chapel. Duke Ellington appeared with his band and the "Father of the Blues," William C. Handy, came to tea at Portia's home. Noble Sissle, whom Portia had first seen during that exciting summer of 1927 in New York, brought his orchestra down for a lively session of his particular brand of jazz. Theatrical performances were less frequent occurrences but Richard B. Harrison and the original Broadway cast staged *The Green Pastures* in the school's auditorium.

Visitors of all types were constantly encouraged and invited to come to Tuskegee. Booker had initiated this policy which some twenty years after his death saw the arrival of his old nemesis, Dr. W. E. B. Du Bois. A party was held in his honor and the dapper Dr. Du Bois danced with every lady in the room. When it came Portia's turn, she said to him, "This is history, isn't it? I wish I had a picture of this to send to the Boston *Guardian* [Monroe Trotter's newspaper]." Du Bois broke up in laughter and during the rest of the evening he charmed her into a great liking for him.

By the early 1940s, Tuskegee Institute had taken on the feverish air that was sweeping the rest of the nation as the world was being battered by yet another great war. A separate, segregated Army pilot training program for blacks was established near Tuskegee, with the Institute receiving a contract from the War Department to administer the ground training program. The first class of five airmen received its wings March 7, 1942. Benjamin O. Davis, Jr., a West Point graduate, former ROTC instructor at Tuskegee, and son of the Army's first black general, was the first to get his wings. Before the war was over, six hundred blacks would become pilots, most of them trained at Tuskegee.

Portia welcomed this influx of new blood into the

Tuskegee community with open arms. Her house became one of the main gathering places for the young airmen and their dates, with Fannie always ready to provide the music for dancing.

But even though most of Portia's time since she left the Tuskegee faculty was taken up between entertaining and teaching a full complement of piano students at her private school, she grew restless for a larger experience. She had returned to Framingham Normal School in 1939 for its centennial celebration and visited with her old friends at Bradford Junior College.

In 1940 she took part in the celebration surrounding the issue of a commemorative stamp bearing Booker T.'s likeness. The U. S. Postmaster General, James A. Farley, made a nationwide radio speech from Tuskegee on the day the stamp went on sale. Musical programs featuring Paul Robeson and Roland Hayes were broadcast from the major American cities. However, this honor to the Tuskegee founder was less than it could have been. The stamp was of the then rarely used ten cent denomination, a compromise measure made to soothe southern congressmen. According to *Life* magazine, there was an attempt to placate the black voting population who remembered the obscure stamp by the later issuance of a "13th Amendment" stamp—just before the 1944 presidential election.

This posthumous honor pleased Portia because she feared the world was quickly forgetting her father and his great work. Many of the people who had been his staunchest supporters were passing from the scene. Robert Moton died in 1940 and three years later she was to mourn the death of her father's admired colleague, Dr. George Washington Carver. Carver's demise occasioned a national outpouring of sorrow, but Portia felt she had lost a dear personal friend. Carver was the classic absent-minded professor—Portia recalled how her daughter Fannie would teasingly ask him for money when she would encounter him on the Tuskegee campus. Pleading poverty, Carver would still rifle through his pockets for loose change, finding instead months of back pay checks that he had neglected to cash.

This anecdote illustrates perfectly the lack of concern Carver possessed for worldly goods. Born around 1859, the son of slaves, on a farm near Diamond Grove, Missouri, he was raised by a white man whose name he assumed. He was consumed, from childhood on, by an interest in plants. He worked his way through school and graduated in 1894 from Iowa State College, where he remained as an assistant botanist until invited by Booker T. Washington to come to Tuskegee in 1896. Through his work in his Tuskegee laboratory he revolutionized the agriculture of the South. He developed products from sweet potatoes, peanuts, and pecans, the formulas for which he gave freely to the world. He made synthetic marble from wood shavings, dyes from clay and starch, gum and wallboard from cotton stalks. Little profit redounded to him personally from his genius, but the world acknowledged his contributions to science. Since his death, public schools in black communities throughout the nation have been named for him, and January 5, the date of his death, has been designated by Congress as George Washington Carver Day.

Before he died, Carver confided in Portia that Booker had wanted him to marry her but that he felt she was too sophisticated for a recluse scientist. Portia was amused at this unknown possibility, but Sidney Pittman was to be the only man, after her father, that she was to love in a significant way. She had a brief affair during her last Tuskegee years with a member of the faculty, Charles Winter Wood. She had been attracted to him because of the fame he had enjoyed during a brief run as "De Lawd" in the 1935 Broadway production of *The Green Pastures*. But nothing serious came of the relationship and Portia was more than content with her life of independence.

In 1944, at the age of sixty-one, Portia retired from all active teaching. She was in excellent health and possessing still the keen intelligence and adventurous spirit which had always kept her in creative motion. She loved Tuskegee and would write to her New England friends of the beauty of the campus and the great progress being made. But she was not at ease there and she closed the doors of her private school with her mind set to finding something else.

She had come across a newspaper notice that the farm in Franklin County, Virginia, which had been her father's birthplace was to be sold at auction. It struck Portia that here was a golden opportunity to restore her father's name to public attention by securing the place where he was born and making some kind of memorial out of it. She feared that the world was forgetting Booker Washington and what she saw as his continuing mission. In 1943 she had watched with sadness the transfer of her father's voluminous collection of private papers from Tuskegee to the Library of Congress where they lay unpublished and nearly forgotten—a situation that was to prevail for the next thirty years. Portia became determined that such oblivion would not befall her father's birthplace. Just as Booker had had a plan for his daughter, Portia now dedicated herself to a plan for her father.

5

Fight the Good Fight

Portia's plan for saving her father's birthplace began in 1944 with her contacting some of his former associates. One of the first persons approached was a man living near her in Tuskegee, Sidney J. Phillips. Phillips was a Tuskegee graduate and, at one time, an agronomy instructor there. He was currently a promotional representative for the Royal Crown Cola Company. Portia knew of his business contacts and it was Royal that agreed to back Phillips' bidding at the auction.

Phillips was a man of large ideas, who not only bid successfully on the birthplace itself, but on the entire 207 acreage comprising the original Burroughs farm. His plan was to set up a Booker T. Washington memorial in Franklin County that would rival any monument erected to a great American. Portia was thrilled by his vision and in a letter she sent to a local newspaper endorsed his plan with gratitude. In the published letter she stated that the Tuskegee authorities had been given first choice in the purchase of the Virginia site but had refused the option, claiming that they were not interested. She wrote, "S. J. Phillips is doing more than is [any] other person of our group to keep the name, Booker T. Washington, before the American people."

The Tuskegee authorities took exception to Portia's statement. They denied not being interested but said they pre-

ferred to keep all of their limited resources for the mainte-
nance of the Institute as a living memorial to Booker. Portia
was roundly criticized on the campus. In explaining the controversy to Dr. Martin F. O'Connor, president of Framingham, Portia wrote: "It is political and unfortunate that I
should always be a victim—however my father was so good
—and the honor to him has made all of us so happy—that I
should overlook personal slights and think only of him . . .
This [Portia's statement about Phillips] is true—and of course
our president of Tuskegee took exception and doesn't feel
friendly toward me. Well such things happen in life and I
must be strong enough to face every issue."

Portia's letter was to prove very prophetic. With the dedication of her life to a public crusade to keep her father's
memory alive, she would open herself as never before to the
capriciousness in human behavior. She would come to see
herself as beleaguered and bedeviled by petty backbiters on
all sides. She believed that they were jealous of her background and influence.

It is unlikely that she would have been dissuaded even if
she had known what lay ahead. Struggle only reinforced her
commitment. Booker had had to struggle against great odds
and outspoken criticism. As his daughter, she believed it
was her mission to shoulder the burden with the same lack
of rancor that had been Booker's mark. Spitefulness was
time consuming and Portia felt herself too busy carrying on
her father's work to engage in such petty behavior. She was
not immune to the attacks of her detractors, but she kept
them at bay, at least psychologically, by an unshakable con-
viction of the rightness and necessity of carrying on Booker
T. Washington's mission.

The plan got off to a start with the incorporation in 1945
of the Booker T. Washington Birthplace Memorial at Rocky
Mount, the nearest large town in Franklin County. Phillips

was made president and Emmett J. Scott, Booker's long-time associate, was called to be the corporation's secretary. The board of trustees that was assembled included, among others, a few old-line Tuskegeeites, Portia, and her nephew Booker III. What they had was 207 acres of land, several broken down old cabins, and a dream. The dream was to restore the site as a shrine and to establish there the Booker T. Washington School of Industrial Training.

The plan for the industrial school came straight from Booker's teachings about the dignity of labor and the "cast-down-your-buckets" philosophy. Almost as if the clock had been turned back to the time Booker left Hampton, a new black educational institution was being planned in terms of bricklaying, carpentry, agriculture, and domestic science. Perhaps Phillips was as strict a disciple of the Washington philosophy as his proposal for a vocationally oriented memorial would suggest. He had been born the son of a Pike Road, Alabama, sharecropper who himself had been persuaded to give up laboring for others and purchase his own farm after attending farm demonstrations at Tuskegee. The greater independence and higher standard of living of his family that resulted from this action could not have been lost on Phillips.

However, it is possible to speculate that Phillips was a shrewd man who understood the temper of the times and what kind of black ventures would succeed. Just as after the Civil War and World War I, there was a "Negro problem" in post-World War II America. Black soldiers returned home demanding the fruits of democracy for which they had fought and died. Blacks were leaving the played-out farms of the South and crowding into northern cities, seeking opportunities that only partially existed. Racial conflict was rampant—there had been eight major race riots in the United States between 1942 and 1946.

Portia

The time was ripe for a project devoted to assisting "the masses of Negroes," a Booker T. Washington Memorial brochure stated, "to become proficient in those qualities and virtues without which they can never become strong Americans . . . qualities such as dependability, cleanliness, honesty, efficiency, loyalty, self-control, etc."

The Virginia General Assembly responded on March 16, 1946, by voting an appropriation of $15,000 toward the Memorial's goals. Governors from forty-two states issued endorsements. The drive was off to a flying start and certainly was not harmed when, on May 23, 1946, a bust of Booker T. Washington was ceremoniously installed in the Hall of Fame in New York.

Portia attended the unveiling, proudly receiving the cloth mantle that had covered the bronze likeness. She was accompanied by her niece, Gloria Davidson Washington, who was a student at Howard University, and her oldest son, Sidney, Jr. Portia was deeply moved by the bust and congratulated the sculptor, Richmond Barthe, for his insight into her father's nature. Barthe, the first black sculptor represented in the Hall of Fame, had devoted three months to creating the piece and considered it one of his best works.

However, the Memorial was to get little direct mileage out of this event. The New York *Times*'s report on the unveiling does not even mention Portia. Tuskegee and Hampton had raised the $5,000 necessary for erecting the bust and were, appropriately, running the show. A memorial concert was held in conjunction with the unveiling several days later at the New York City Center. Among its patrons were the leading lights of the black and white cultural communities of New York. The net proceeds from the concert were slated for the United Negro College Fund, which had been founded by Tuskegee's President Patterson in 1944.

The Memorial had a bolder plan for raising money. Encouraged by their success with the Virginia legislature, the corporation set out to capture the support of the ultimate source of public funds, the United States Congress.

Their approach was to be shrewdly pragmatic while at the same time imaginatively sentimental. Congress was called upon to enact a bill, as follows:

> To authorize the coinage of 50-cent pieces to commemorate the life and perpetuate the ideals and teachings of Booker T. Washington . . . Such coins may be disposed of at par or at a premium by banks or trust companies selected by the Booker T. Washington Birthplace Memorial of Franklin County, Virginia, and all proceeds therefrom shall be used to purchase, construct, and maintain suitable memorials to the memory of Booker T. Washington, deceased, as may be decided upon by the Booker T. Washington Birthplace Memorial of Virginia.

A representative from Virginia, Thomas G. Burch, introduced the bill into the House, where it was passed July 15, 1946. On July 23 it was considered at a hearing before the Senate Committee on Banking and Currency. Phillips, Emmett Scott, and Portia's nephew Booker III appeared to give testimony. While Phillips and Scott emphasized the worthiness of the bill, the younger Booker III was almost embarrassingly candid in his views: "This coin . . . is a source of revenue for this organization and it is that that we need. We have so few ways of getting money to carry on things of this kind. Philanthropy as it was in the days when Tuskegee was built has sort of dwindled away and we have to use a practical means of getting money to carry on works of this kind."

The only major objection was raised by the assistant general counsel of the Treasury Department, Stephen J. Spingarn. He voiced fears that the enactment of legislation providing for this commemorative coin honoring "a great American leader" would open the gates to a flood of such coins, thus resulting in widespread abuse to the U.S. coinage system. The counsel proposed, instead, that the Bureau of the Mint be directed to issue a commemorative medal. This alternative proposal was rejected, with the coin bill being passed by the unanimous consent of the Senate committee.

Portia remembered those days on Capitol Hill as hard but heady work. Wherever Phillips told her to go, Portia went. Before getting the bill through Congress, the two of them saw nearly every Congressman and Senator on the Hill. Many displayed great sympathy for their cause and most were at least willing to listen to their pitch. Even President Harry Truman was not exempt from their determination. He was to become quite familiar with the sound of Mrs. Portia Washington Pittman's bouncy step as she sought entrance to the Oval Office yet another time.

Finally, on August 7, 1946, President Truman signed the bill authorizing the minting of five million Booker T. Washington commemorative 50-cent coins. Present at the signing were the chief officers of the Memorial, Sidney Phillips and Emmett Scott.

Portia was jubilant; it was the first time since the Dallas chorus that she had really felt on top of the world. She saw a whole new chapter of her life opening up before her and plunged into it with the fervor that was so characteristically hers. Phillips arranged for her to move from Tuskegee to Roanoke, Virginia, so as to be near the Franklin County memorial site. She was integral to the fund-raising effort and raised on her own nearly $11,000 in one year through the sale of the commemorative coins to friends and acquaintances on whom she personally called in Virginia, Maryland, and Washington, D.C.

Every sign pointed to success for the drive for the Memorial fund. Letters and checks had begun to pour in before the bill had even cleared the Senate. The number of gubernatorial endorsements increased to encompass all the states in the Union. The Southern Newspapers Publishers' Association put their organization on record in support of it at their annual convention. Mayor William O'Dwyer of New York personally kicked off the drive in the city.

Although there was general endorsement by black organizations of the honor being paid to Booker himself, the industrial school concept received only lukewarm acknowledgment. Even where there was black interest, the fact that the Memorial was authorized to sell the commemorative coin for $1.00 meant that a large majority of blacks would find the spending of a dollar for 50 cents' worth of purchasing power economically impossible. Clearly, to succeed, the campaign to build the school had to be conducted in the spirit of a grand interracial undertaking of mutual benefit to both races. Black youth would be uplifted, war veterans taken off the streets, and new consumers created for the American economy.

Portia supported these goals fully. Like her father before her, most of her experience with black people had been in the South. She believed that vocational education was the solution for the problems of rural blacks, which was not necessarily incorrect for the time and place. What she still had to reckon with was the new breed of northern blacks.

But politics had always bored Portia and she chose to ignore any distractions from her glorious campaign. A competition was held for the design of the coin; it was won by the sculptor Isaac Hathaway, making him the first black to design a United States coin. Once the coin was minted and Portia had exhausted her local Virginia contacts, she headed straight for New England where, with elaborate ceremony, she presented a coin to the president of Framington, Dr. Martin O'Connor, in April of 1948. This stop was the beginning for her of a six-week tour of the Boston area. Arrangements for the tour had been made by the Jordan Marsh Company, a large and prestigious Boston department store. Once again Portia had brought together the chemistry of the Booker T. Washington name with contacts cultivated since her school days.

Sidney Phillips knew he had a valuable ally in Booker's daughter, and Portia recalled that he always provided her with a pleasant traveling companion, even at times sending his own secretary, Miss Monday. On her Boston trip she was accompanied by a young man named Walter Mason Roper. Roper was a baritone soloist who would provide musical entertainment at their stops. Since their goal was the distribution of 200,000 coins, Portia was glad for all the help she could get.

The spring of 1948 was nearly over when Portia finally returned to the house she maintained in Tuskegee, the Roanoke move having been only temporary until the Memorial campaign got off the ground. She wrote to Bradford Junior College, thanking the president, Dorothy M. Bell, for sending a contribution:

Tuskegee Inst. Ala.
June 21, 48

My Dear Miss Bell:—
After an extensive tour of twenty-eight states, I am at home for a few days trying to clean house and catch up with my correspondence.
Thank you for your contribution. We do appreciate

each donation, because it is quite a struggle—as you probably realize.

I was disappointed not to have met you—and the B.A. girls, so that I might have explained to them as I did at other schools—I hope to return in the fall and I shall let you know early enough.

Please thank your secretary and the other young lady for their courtesy. It was a real pleasure to see the wonderful new buildings and all the changes. I shall always feel grateful to Bradford for the many things it did for me and I shall look forward with real pleasure towards meeting you.

With fondest regards—
I am

Yours sincerely,
Portia W. Pittman

By the following year, 1949, Portia had taken up residence in Washington, D.C., with her son, Sidney, Jr. Fannie had married and moved to Kansas City, and there seemed to Portia little reason to remain in Tuskegee. With the seeming success of the Memorial campaign, her life at Tuskegee had become even less tenable. The move had been urged by Phillips because it would cut down on some of the distance she traveled for the Memorial. It was with few regrets that she closed the door on that phase of her life and headed North.

The work of the Memorial staff had begun to bear fruit. Roads were constructed into the site and a replica of the slave cabin where Booker lived had been erected. Portia remembered the day of the dedication in May 1949 when she choked with emotion as she cut the ribbon and received the key from the governor of Virginia, William M. Tuck.

Additional land adjacent to the birthplace site was acquired, some six hundred acres, and put under cultivation. A night trade school was established on the new land, with a branch named the Booker T. Washington Memorial Trade School being opened soon after in Roanoke. Phillips claimed it as the only private trade school in Virginia certified to train veterans under the G.I. Bill. There was an extension service that through publications, a weekly radio program, and the establishment of community service clubs, hoped to enlighten the South about the Memorial's health, good will, and "loyalty" programs. As for this last point, Phillips seems to have been an ardent anticommunist. Half of the income from the sale of the memorial coins in 1951 had been earmarked by him "to fight communism among Negroes." But by then it was the beginning of the McCarthy period and Phillips could have been hedging his bets against the House Un-American Activities Committee's looking with any suspicion upon his organization.

The first visible cracks in this rosy picture of achievement appeared with the introduction of a bill on January 3, 1951, in the House of Representatives. The bill was "to provide for the establishment of a veterans' hospital for Negro veterans at the birthplace of Booker T. Washington in Franklin County, Virginia" with the sum of $5 million. The bill was sponsored by Representative John Rankin (Democrat, Mississippi), with the quiet endorsement of Sidney J. Phillips.

All hell broke loose on the House floor, led by a fiery young black representative from New York, Adam Clayton Powell, Jr. Powell blasted the bill as a "Jim Crow" measure to segregate black veterans and black medical personnel. He was supported in his stand by the only other black representative in Congress, William L. Dawson (Democrat, Illinois), the NAACP, and thirty other national organizations concerned with civil rights. A number of white congressmen also came forward in opposition. Representative Emanuel Celler (Democrat, New York) took exception to Rankin's use in debate of the term "nigra" instead of Negro. Rankin shot back that Negroes preferred to be called "nigras." The bill was defeated in the House in June, by a vote of 222 to 117.

Powell went further, to demand that there be a congressional investigation of the Memorial foundation, branding it a "phony organization." He charged that 90 per cent of the profits from the sale of the memorial coin had gone to pay salaries. Phillips was personally attacked by Powell as being without the slightest stature in the black community. Tuskegee Institute had never endorsed the Memorial foundation, Powell said, nor had any other prominent black organization or individual.

Phillips denied the accusations, stoutly defending the Memorial and the good it had done. However, there had never been any public accounting of the $600,000 which Phillips acknowledged having raised by the sale of over a million memorial coins. Furthermore, a mysterious fire had occurred at the memorial site at the end of 1950 resulting in the destruction of the records housed there of some three million names of people who had contributed to the Memorial.

Portia, in an exclusive interview with the Chicago *Defender*, June 23, 1951, revealed that she had withdrawn from the Memorial organization some eighteen months previous. She stated that she had been dissatisfied with the business methods used by Phillips in running the Memorial. All other members of the Washington family who had been involved, as well as Emmett Scott, had also withdrawn from the foundation.

Time has blurred the exact details of Portia's split with the Phillips organization, but it seems to have been a painless one. She never doubted his esteem for her father or that he worked diligently to preserve the Washington memory. They remained friends and were even to work together again in the future. However, Adam Clayton Powell, Jr., was forever to be her nemesis even though she had not supported the Rankin bill in 1951.

By 1954, the Booker T. Washington Birthplace Memorial was in debt for $140,000. One theory of the day held that Phillips' board of trustees consisted, with one black exception, of the white members of Congress who had put through the commemorative coin bill in 1946 and a few white big businessmen who allowed their names to be used for fund-raising purposes but otherwise took little interest in the Memorial's operation. Thus, the Memorial's financial situation was allowed to get completely out of hand through poor management before the board stepped in. All activities were suspended and, on February 26, 1955, the birthplace site and all other accumulated lands and buildings were put on sale to the highest bidder.

First in line at the auction was Mrs. Portia Washington Pittman. Phillips had come to her aid again. From among people who still believed in the memorial idea, he raised $16,000, which enabled Portia to purchase the original 207 acreage of the Burroughs farm.

Plans for the birthplace property were vague, but they had had to move so swiftly to secure the property. But its fate did not hang in the balance long. Phillips and Portia went back into the lobbying business. They brought the Commonwealth of Virginia and the U. S. Congress together in an agreement that the former would pay Portia $17,000 for the property and donate it to the federal government if the latter would enact legislation making the birthplace a national monument. Congress moved swiftly on the proposal. By April of the following year, 1956, the national monument was authorized with an allocation of $200,000. There was a reproduction of the log cabin in which Booker was born; a visitor's center was constructed and winding trails laid out through the old Burroughs plantation. Portia was present when the ribbon was cut at the opening of the Booker T. Washington National Monument, July 27, 1957.

In reflecting back over the long battle, Portia said: "The government has it now, we had the government buy the place. And it's kept up beautifully. So I'm very proud of the fact that we labored to get it, so that it wouldn't be sold at auction to just any and everybody."

Portia and Phillips went their separate ways but remained joined in their dedication to perpetuating Booker's memory. Phillips set up a new organization to commemorate the one hundredth anniversary of Booker's birth in 1956. Congress passed a supplemental bill to the one creating the national monument that included an item designating $225,000 for Phillips' Centennial Commission. A Booker T. Washington centennial postage stamp was also issued to mark the occasion.

Portia, upon her quiet withdrawal from the ill-fated Birthplace Memorial organization, had established the Booker T. Washington Foundation. She drew together an illustrious group of names for the board of governors and, taking no chances this time, assumed the office of treasurer-general herself. General Ulysses Grant III, the vice president of George Washington University, was head of the board which comprised several senators, a congressman, and Mrs. Alice Roosevelt Longworth.

Alice Longworth's friendship with Portia extended back over many years to the time her father, Teddy Roosevelt, had been President. Portia delighted in recounting the following story told to her by her good friend: "One day Teddy Roosevelt said, 'Alice, I've been criticized for your smoking in the house. I don't ever want you to smoke another cigarette in the house as long as I'm President.' 'All right, Daddy, I won't.' Then she got up, put on some old clothes, went up to the roof, and smoked. And he said, 'What are you doing up on the roof?' 'Well, you told me I couldn't smoke in the house!'"

The idea for the Foundation had come to Portia because of her involvement with the High Mowing School, a private academy in Wilton, New Hampshire. She had been invited by a former Bradford classmate to visit the school, a visit which resulted in at least six black boys and girls receiving scholarships to attend High Mowing. One of these students was the granddaughter of Portia's niece Nettie. Of historical interest was this niece's marriage to Frederick Douglass III, thus intermingling the blood of the two most influential black leaders of their day.

Frederick Douglass had died in 1895, just at the time Booker T. Washington was beginning his ascendancy to power. Booker acknowledged a spiritual debt to Douglass even though their lives were to follow very different courses. Douglass was a runaway slave who came to international prominence as a powerful speaker in the abolitionist movement. Never one for accommodation, he actively provoked confrontation with the white superstructure and strove throughout his lifetime to secure the rights of full citizenship for American blacks. Had he lived, he would have opposed the Washington doctrine. In death, his name became bound together with Booker T. Washington's as the leaders of their race.

While the Booker T. Washington Foundation's main activity was securing scholarship aid for black students (Portia said they granted more than $18,000 in aid their first year and a half in business), it also was involved with such diverse undertakings as trying to organize a boys' club in Maryland and construct a thirteen-room motel for blacks in the then highly segregated District of Columbia. Neither of these projects materialized, so Portia concentrated her full attention on scholarship activities.

Preference for scholarships was given to students planning to pursue careers in medicine. This bias was Portia's wish because neither her mother, Fanny, nor her father had enjoyed good health; even after all these years, she still brooded over what she considered the premature deaths of her parents. The scholarships were granted with the stipulation that the recipients had "to toil for part of their keep." By requiring that, Portia believed, the education would be earned in a way her father would have approved. With each passing year, she had become more committed to what she described as "carrying on my father's mission." Age, rather than diminishing her fervor, only seemed to increase it.

Wherever she traveled she carried copies of her father's books. She left some to be sold in the Bradford Junior college bookstore on a visit there in 1951. She had to discipline herself not to give them away, which would have been her natural inclination. But she was working now for the Foundation and her finances were slim.

Her richest resource was the Washington name. The flurry of activity in the mid-1950s to memorialize Booker was a shot in the arm for the Foundation. Despite the controversy and the questions raised about some of S. J. Phillips' methods, the Booker T. Washington National Monument was established, Virginia Highway 122 renamed the BTW Memorial Highway, and a BTW centennial stamp issued, all due to his activities. The money voted by Congress for Phillips' Centennial Commission enabled Portia to travel. In a letter to the president of Framingham, she wrote:

> . . . This is the Centennial year of my father's [birth] and Congress made a fine contribution for us to use in

spreading his philosophy. I have worked very hard visiting different states, speaking, etc. and tomorrow is my birthday. I shall be seventy-four years of age and I am grateful to God for almost perfect health and that I am able to work in His Vineyard.

Sidney, Portia's husband, was not faring as well. After a long illness, he died in a Dallas hospital, February 19, 1958. Portia and Fannie journeyed to Dallas for the church funeral and were duly acknowledged, along with Booker and Sidney, Jr., as the only surviving relatives. Portia felt it was only proper to attend; after all, he was the father of her children but she did not regret her decision of almost thirty years before to end the marriage. "He was such a brilliant man, but so bitter. It was bitterness that killed him," Portia contended. But to give Sidney some credit, he did manage to keep going to the ripe old age of eighty-two.

Fannie was by this time Mrs. Alphonso Marcelle Kennedy. She had married a physician and was living in Kansas City, Missouri. While Portia's relationship with Fannie was very close and Sidney, Jr., was her living companion, it was to be her son Booker that was to come back into her life with the excitement on which she had always thrived.

Booker had left Europe in 1936 with the Brazilian pianist Romeo Silva, to open the Casino Atlantico in Rio de Janeiro. The following year he went to Buenos Aires with his own group, the Swing Stars. He built a small but devoted following that kept him working there ten years. Some consider him *the* man who "exported" jazz to South America. But an Argentinian law that required thirty minutes of Argentinian music to be played for every fifteen minutes of foreign music finally drove the jazzman back to Brazil, only to find that gambling had been banned which resulted in the closing of the casino.

Booker then dropped out of sight giving rise to rumors that he was drying out, strung out, or dead. "They had it out all over America that Booker Pittman was dead," Portia remembered with pain. "I knew Booker wasn't dead. I just felt it, although he wouldn't write to me." The truth was that Booker had become a drug addict. Portia was never to know how long her son used heroin, but she was not surprised when she learned that it was only after his habit threatened to wreck the one sustaining force in his life, his music, that he pulled himself back from the brink of destruction.

With the closing of the casinos in the late 1940s, Booker and his fellow jazzmen found it difficult getting work in Rio. There were a few private parties and small club dates, but these jobs were slight compared to the engagements they had previously enjoyed. During one of these appearances, Booker was approaching the bandstand when he slumped to the floor in a drug-induced stupor. When he regained his senses, he found himself bruised, bloodied, and banned from the club. Then and there Booker determined that he had to remove himself as far as possible away from drugs and the influences that kept him using them. He retreated into the Brazilian interior to a small coffee town named Santo Antônio de Platina, where, a stranger and alone, he broke the habit. Booker embraced his clean, new life of obscurity and remained in Santo Antônio for ten years.

His bohemian life came to an end when he was persuaded by Philipe Corcodel, a perfume salesman and amateur trombonist, to come out of retirement. In the fall of 1956 Corcodel was passing through Santo Antônio and by accident overheard Booker playing folk music. He immediately recognized the jazzman's style and was thunderstruck because he had accepted the reports on Booker's death. The jazz world was not to be denied and in short order Booker's ca-

reer was again on the rise. In 1959 he recorded an album for
RCA entitled *Booker Plays Again*. Portia kept the album
cover on display, pointing to it with pride as an example of a
lost man who came back, an example she believed it would
behoove the youth of today to study.

In 1962 Booker returned to the United States in triumph.
He was invited by Jack Paar, who had heard him play in
Brazil, to appear on his TV show. He was accompanied to
the States by his black Brazilian wife, Ofelia, and his stepdaughter, Eliana. Booker and Ofelia, who was a widow, had
met in 1957 in Louis Armstrong's dressing room in Rio de
Janeiro. She had introduced a note of stability into Booker's
life that eased his transition back into the public eye. In
describing his years of absence in Santo Antônio, Booker
said that he spent them "drinking rum, living the good life,
and playing and singing Brazilian folk music." Now, he was
a teetotaler and jazzman *par excellence*.

Portia and Fannie traveled to New York in 1962 for a joy-
ful reunion with the prodigal son. Ofelia, even though
speaking little English, endeared herself to Portia, who
remembered her daughter-in-law warmly as being a kind
and solid person. She said of her son, "I didn't want him to
go back, but that was where he had been most popular and
he owed it to his family." Eliana had a budding singing and
acting career of her own in Brazil. She and Booker put together an act that was successfully received in the States.
But in Brazil, they were nationally known in their own
right, and at the end of the summer of 1962 Booker returned
to his adopted country with his family.

Portia mourned the departure of her son, but life in
Washington held its diversions. She was constantly being
visited by members of her family, now far flung, old friends
from the Bradford and Framingham days, and Tuskegee
people. She traveled often to Kansas City to see Fannie and

was written up by the local press there when a Booker T. Washington monument was unveiled in Malden, West Virginia, Booker's boyhood home, in 1963. It was a granite bust set against a pylon of granite on a 400-foot frontage on U. S. Highway 60. Although eighty years of age, Portia attended the ceremony along with West Virginia's governor and former governor and some fifteen hundred guests.

Two years later, Booker returned from Brazil for a brief tour of the States. He appeared with Eliana at the Playboy Club in Kansas City and hung out with many of his old buddies in Atlanta and New York. American jazz had taken on new dimensions that Booker did not completely understand. He recognized that his brand of jazz, highly influenced by southern blues and Dixieland, was on the wane. In its place was the music born of urban ghetto experience and the funk of close living and raucous city sounds. Still, he felt comfortable with the new music because in all its innovativeness and "coolness," it was still based on the black sound he had helped pioneer.

The next four years of Portia's life were to be the saddest she had ever known. And as she had so often in the past, she turned to her New England acquaintances for strength and comfort. On May 26, 1967, she wrote to Miss Bell at Bradford on the back of a blank check: "I have just lost my oldest child Sidney, Jr. . . . I am in a kind of shock."

Of her three children, Sidney, Jr., had been the solid, steady one, just like her father. His death left her empty and alone in Washington. Fannie came to grieve with her and together they journeyed back to Kansas City. But within two years, they were to make the trip back to Washington, now both widows. They say things come in threes. For Portia, the triptych of her tragedy was complete with Booker's death from cancer in a Saõ Paulo hospital in 1969.

"D.C. VISIT REVEALS BOOKER T. WASHINGTON'S CHILD IN POV-

ERTY" read the title of an article published in the July 23, 1970, issue of *Jet* magazine. At eighty-seven years of age, Portia was residing in a tiny, roach-infested apartment in a Washington tenement, located in a district having the fourth highest crime rate in the city. Her neighbors were the poor and the dispirited. Junkies shot up in the surrounding apartments where children slept three in a bed. The threat of robbery kept her two and one-half rooms wrapped in gloom. The windows were locked shut and heavily draped against the repetition of the night she awoke to find a burglar casing her kitchen window with a flashlight. Her screams drove that intruder away but she was not always so lucky.

Crueler acts were perpetrated by people who gained her confidence and were invited through the front door. A "preacher" took a bag of dirty laundry, never to be seen again. Two friendly young men ran off with a briefcase stuffed with clippings she had been saving for a scrapbook. But cruelest of all were the people who visited under the guise of celebrating Booker T. Washington's daughter. They often pilfered things from the meager collection of mementos that remained to her.

Tuskegee had offered the daughter of its founder a home at the Institute. Portia refused it, preferring her life of independence in the city. For in spite of her age, she felt strong and mentally alert enough to take care of herself: "I haven't the sense to know I'm getting old." She still believed then that she had to carry on her father's work, and a return to Tuskegee, so greatly changed now, would diminish this effort as well as her own individuality.

She would have preferred better surroundings, but her resources were very limited now. The Booker T. Washington memorials and stamps and commemorative coins were long forgotten by the world. His work doctrine and supposed

"Uncle Tom" social philosophy had been dishonored and buried by the civil rights movement, itself by then in ashes. Portia had to make her way on a $300-a-month pension from Tuskegee, social security benefits, and a small annual royalty payment from her father's autobiography, *Up from Slavery*. She shared this meager income with Fannie, who had exhausted her widow's benefits and, through failing health, had become semi-invalid.

The building had been much nicer when they moved there years before. Even though the intervening years had seen its rapid deterioration, it was still someplace familiar where Portia was well known. Being known was always very important to Portia. As long as she had an audience she could choose to ignore anything negative in her surroundings.

She received visitors as if she were ensconced in one of the grand houses she had known in Europe. Of course, there were not so many now, but Bradford continued to keep up with her and there were historians and journalists who periodically sought her out. All found her charming, gracious, and eager to talk. For Portia, the Booker T. Washington saga was as fresh as it had ever been. She would recite passages from the Atlanta speech of 1895, remembering how her father had practiced that speech over and over again on her as a child. She would talk of her own life, saying that she had no regrets and would rather be the poor daughter of Booker T. Washington than a rich daughter of the wealthiest man on earth. No, Portia had no regrets. Money had always been like quicksilver in her hands and it was not in her nature to mourn being without it. Something always came along to relieve the grim realities of her life, and in April of 1970 it was a trip to the White House.

Mrs. Portia Washington Pittman was invited to lunch with Robert J. Brown, the black assistant to President

Richard Nixon at that time. While it was very political on the part of the Administration, Portia found it good entertainment. The newspapers gave great play to her support of Nixon's desegregation policies while ignoring the highly integrated life she had lived. Portia, of course, had been to the White House before the then still in favor Richard Nixon was even born. She had seen too much history not to know when to project a conservative image. Booker would have been proud.

Privately, Portia was more candid about her true feelings: "White people have to be watched. A white man will steal a railroad and eventually get caught. A Negro will steal a chicken and get caught immediately and get the same punishment. . . . I called up Governor George Wallace [of Alabama] after he had been shot [in 1972]. He always used to say, 'Portia, you get the colored people to vote for me and I'll look after Tuskegee.' I played up to him because he could do a lot for the school . . . I called up Senator Stennis' office after he was shot [in 1973]. It's not catering to them [whites] but we have to live together down there. We need to keep friends 'cause they can do us a lot of harm. My papa would say to the colored people who criticized his Atlanta speech, 'Make sense with these people because it's both our Southland. We've both got to come up together. It's yours; if they are destroyed, then you are really destroyed. You can't work without them, and they can't work without you!'"

Portia made no apologies for Booker's notorious speech delivered at Atlanta. She believed that even today Booker would have said, "Cast down your buckets where you are." Blacks had made great progress since then and she recognized that things were different than they were in her father's time. But she still believed that it was necessary to start at the bottom and build a strong practical foundation before scaling the heights of ambition. She cited herself and Hazel Harrison and the way they both arrived in Berlin without a firm grounding in technique.

Even though she never lost faith, Portia realized that the Washington philosophy was looked down upon by the more militant blacks. But she believed that in time Booker's position would be reassessed and vindicated. "His idea was to build up the race, through education and training, so that it could meet any challenge. He felt that social equality would come as a result," she said.

When asked by the author about what would have been Booker's position *vis-à-vis* the civil rights movement with its sometime violent sit-ins and "freedom rides," she chuckled: "Booker would have been serious and calm." He would have liked Martin Luther King, Jr., she believed, because he was a down-to-earth black preacher who understood his people's basic needs. Portia liked King and had spent two hours talking with him once at Howard University. King had been a great admirer of W. E. B. Du Bois and Portia regaled him with the story of the ultimate Washington-Du Bois rapprochement when she danced with her father's critic so long ago at Tuskegee.

The ability to laugh at both herself and the world had been one of the traits which enabled Portia to survive her many hard knocks with unshakable optimism. The first real challenge to this optimism came in the fall of 1971 when she suffered a heart attack. She had been having dizzy spells for several days but put them down to the exasperations of old age (she was now eighty-eight). But there came a night when she fell to the floor unable to move except to cry out. She was rushed to Freedmen's Hospital almost given up for dead. She lay in a coma some days before the doctors were able to put a heart pacemaker in her chest. Portia remembered her time there as a nightmare. Doctors came and went, but it was the black nurses that were her particular torment.

They had been put on notice that their patient was not just anybody from the Washington ghetto. Already overworked, her attendants were annoyed that they were being required to give extra attention to an old lady they knew nothing about. "Booker T. Washington, he was just an old peanut man," Portia remembered them saying. Despite her pain, Portia had to laugh.

In their ignorance of their own history, the nurses had confused Booker T. Washington with George Washington Carver. Carver had indeed been the "peanut man," whose many scientific experiments had helped revitalize the agricultural economy of the post-Civil War South. Self-effacing and unambitious in a worldly sense, Carver had derived little financial benefit from his discoveries, which were to be used by other people to make millions of dollars. Ironically, had Portia been his daughter, with her drive things might have turned out differently.

Portia had always had a great liking for the young, but she was a very sick lady. Her defenses were down and the lack of court paid to her by the fledgling nurses left her very embittered. For the first time in her life she began to wonder if it had all been worth it. Here she was, a person who had known the hospitality of Presidents and royalty, the exhilaration of artistic success and the power of an internationally respected heritage, lying bedridden and unacknowledged in a hospital whose very existence, she felt, was made possible by her father's influence on Congress, which authorized the construction of Freedmen's Hospital in 1903.

Her thoughts drifted back, to the reunion with her son Booker on his triumphal return from Brazil, to the successful fight for her father's birthplace memorial, to the six-hundred-voice chorus in Dallas. Fannie attended her in the hospital the best she could, but Portia chose to remember her daughter's earlier musical precociousness and the sound of Fannie's long fingers, now arthritic, beating out the "St. Louis Blues." Berlin came vividly into her mind and she could see *Vom Sklaven Empor (Up from Slavery)* sitting in the most prominent bookstores in the city. Her New England school days were especially sweet to her, with the days spent playing in the Framingham grove and warm visits with her father at Bradford. Her father, her Papa, the "quiet, unassuming person, very tender-hearted, sympathetic and kind" protector who had left her so early in her long life.

Portia drifted through eight months of slow and painful recovery in the hospital. The time finally arrived when she could be moved around in a wheel chair. At the sight of that wheel chair, she was swept by a great wave of emotion. She remembered that her mother had spent the last of her days in a wheel chair. Her mother had always been very real to her even though she had been too young to have really known her. But details culled from her mother's contemporaries and Booker's painful recollections about his first love had provided Portia with food for her always romantic imagination. Over the years she created an image of her mother, Fanny, that she loved with an intensity usually reserved for the living. Now she saw Fanny struggling in her wheel chair to get well. And she saw herself and became determined that her mother's child would make it. And she did. Portia came home.

Mrs. Portia Washington Pittman came home walking. Somewhat slowed in body but still mentally sharp, she reflected upon her long life with pride and gracious good humor. She was expressive in her love of people, giving generously of her time and memories to any who sought her attention. She gave valuable assistance to Dr. Louis R.

Portia

Harlan for his 1972 publication of *The Booker T. Washington Papers,* which was dedicated to her. To the present author, she gave limitless time always accompanied by the demure offer of a cocktail or light repast. Her genteel manner had a more proper setting now, for she and Fannie had been moved into a new apartment, with people to come in and look after them, by the Tuskegee Alumni Club of Washington. Her old upright piano seemed out of place in its modern surroundings, but it still responded to its owner's occasional burst of energetic playing. Music would always be her first love, and even though she admitted to not understanding the modern "stuff," if it gave pleasure to others, then she was "all for it."

There was not much that Portia in her life of nearly a century had let get by her unnoticed. The puritanical Booker would have been shocked at the "new morality" that had evolved since his time, but Portia had taken it in stride. She would still occasionally take a little sherry (having begrudgingly given up scotch) and daintily puff on a cigarette. The fashions of the seventies were outlandish to her, but she liked the fact that people, especially women, were finally able to be comfortable in their clothes. "Women's Liberation" was not a part of her vocabulary but she understood a woman's longing to have a life of her own. She recalled her own unhappiness back in Dallas when she tried to be a domesticated female. She had really wanted to pursue that professional musical career and now summed up herself as having been "a crazy kid" for giving it all up to get married.

But Portia would not tolerate the "if-I-had-only-done-something-else "excuse." She took full responsibility for all of her actions. Things had been made difficult sometimes because of the jealousy she believed certain people felt for her. But, likening herself to her father, she had planned, with dignity and hard work, to overcome them all. In the hospital she had been asked if she were named for "Portia Faces Life," a popular radio soap opera. Laughing at their ignorance, Portia, with a sprinkling of German asides, informed them that she had been named by her father for the "courageous Portia" in *The Merchant of Venice*. "Yes, I have faced life but directly, head on and not like some mythical radio program."

Portia was always a fighter and, after Fannie's death during an epileptic seizure in the fall of 1973, she girded herself to go on fighting alone. Her mainstay as always was her unwavering faith in her father. She was heartened by the thrust generated in the 1960s to rediscover black history, because she felt that any re-examination of the role black people played in America would throw new light on her father and restore his name to prominence. Whether or not the Washington doctrine would be immediately vindicated, Portia was glad that this black reawakening had not come too late for her, because she wanted to be right in the middle of the hue and cry of the debate.

During a recent summer while traveling through Berlin, I found with the aid of old city maps the site of Portia's boarding house. All that she had known in her happy student days there was gone, 58 Steglitzer Strasse now being occupied by a flower shop topped by a five-story prefabricated apartment building. I stood in front of it, sadly reflecting on how different Portia's life might have been had she remained in Germany and completed her studies. She could have become an accomplished musician and enjoyed a life of personal freedom and artistic fulfillment at home and abroad. Or she could have married one of her many white suitors and assumed the peacefully detached life of an expatriate. But no, Portia was the daughter of Booker T. Washington and the power of that special black American heritage preordained that she would live her life as she had.

Portia

Portia Washington Pittman made no apologies for the manner in which she traversed the long history that was uniquely hers. With quiet courage, she had met the challenges and overcome the obstacles to her pursuit of a meaningful life of dedication to her father, to her race, and to her art.

Portia had never looked back and running that day to catch up with my Berlin taxicab driver, grown impatient now that the search for Steglitzer Strasse had ended, I dismissed my wistful speculations and I too did not look back.

Postscript

In the March 15, 1973, issue of the *Wall Street Journal*, an article was featured on the front page that described a "new" approach to higher education which bore a striking resemblance to the Booker T. Washington vocational doctrine. The report focused on the School of the Ozarks (founded 1906), a small liberal arts college located in Point Lookout, Missouri, whose motto is: "Work is love made visible." To quote the *Journal*'s reporter:

> Commitment to the good-old-fashioned work ethic, in fact, runs so deep here that honest toil is an integral part of the curriculum. Students don't pay room, board or tuition here, they work their way through college doing everything from typing tests and mopping floors to driving bulldozers, butchering hogs and selling orchids —and those who shirk their assigned campus jobs flunk out. . . .

Although the School of the Ozarks was small, William W. Gordon, executive vice-president of the Council for Financial Aid to Education Inc., a New York based non-profit organization set up to encourage contributions to higher education, heralded the college as representing "an idea whose time has come. Integrating more occupational education with the liberal arts is an important trend in higher education, and one that has been too long in coming."

If this trend prevails, and recent developments in higher education would seem to argue its success, Portia Washington Pittman's unwavering faith in her father's mission will not have been in vain.

Bibliography

Brawley, Benjamin. *Paul Laurence Dunbar: Poet of His People*. Chapel Hill, University of North Carolina Press, 1936.

Catton, Bruce. *The Savage Ideal: Intolerance and Intellectual Leadership in the South, 1890–1914*. Baltimore, Johns Hopkins University Press, 1972.

Cruder, Robert. *The Negro in Reconstruction*. Englewood Cliffs, N.J., Prentice-Hall, 1969.

Culp, D. W. *Twentieth-Century Negro Literature*. Naperville, Ill., J. L. Nichols, 1902.

Cunard, Nancy, comp. *Negro Anthology, 1931–33*. London, Wishart, 1934.

Drinker, Frederick E. *Booker T. Washington: The Master Mind of a Child of Slavery*. Pamphlet. Memorial Edition, 1915.

Du Bois, W. E. B. *The Autobiography of W. E. B. Du Bois*. New York, International, 1968.

Elliot, Lawrence. *George Washington Carver: The Man Who Overcame*. Englewood Cliffs, N.J., Prentice-Hall, 1966.

Fox, Stephen R. *The Guardian of Boston: William Monroe Trotter*. New York, Atheneum, 1970.

144

Bibliography

Framingham State College. *First State Normal School in America, 1839–1939.* Framingham, Mass., June 1959.

———. *Historical Résumé.* Framingham, Mass., June 1964.

———. *Historical Sketches.* Framingham, Mass., July 1914.

Francis, Charles E. *The Tuskegee Airmen.* Boston, Bruce Humphries, 1955.

Franklin, John Hope. *From Slavery to Freedom,* 3d ed. New York, Knopf, 1967.

Gayle, Addison, Jr. *Oak and Ivy: A Biography of Paul Laurence Dunbar.* Garden City, N.Y., Doubleday, 1971.

Green, Constance M. *The Secret City: A History of Race Relations in the National Capital.* Princeton, N.J., Princeton University Press, 1967.

Haley, James T., comp. *Afro-American Encyclopedia.* Nashville, Tenn., Haley & Florida, 1896.

Handlin, Oscar, ed. *Race and Nationality in American Life.* Boston, Little, Brown, 1957.

Harlan, Louis R. *Booker T. Washington: The Making of a Black Leader, 1856–1901.* New York, Oxford, 1972.

Harlan, Louis R., and John W. Blassingame, eds. *The Booker T. Washington Papers,* Vols. I, II. Urbana, Ill., University of Illinois Press, 1972.

Hartshorn, W. N., ed. *An Era of Progress and Promise, 1863–1910.* Boston, Priscilla Publishing Co., 1910.

Hughes, William H., and Frederick D. Patterson, eds. *Robert Russa Moton of Hampton and Tuskegee.* Chapel Hill, University of North Carolina Press, 1956.

Mackintosh, Barry. *Booker T. Washington: An Appreciation of the Man and His Times.* Washington, D.C., U. S. Dept. of the Interior, 1972.

145

Bibliography

Mathews, Basil. *Booker T. Washington.* Cambridge, Mass., Harvard University Press, 1948.

National Encyclopedia of the Colored Races, Vol. I. Montgomery, Ala., National Publishing Co., 1919.

Robeson, Paul. *Here I Stand.* New York, Othello Associates, 1958.

Sayers, W. C. B. *Samuel Coleridge-Taylor: Musician.* London, Cassell, 1915.

Scott, Emmett J., and Lyman B. Stowe. *Booker T. Washington.* London, T. Fisher Unwin, 1916.

Spencer, Samuel R., Jr. *Booker T. Washington and the Negro's Place in American Life.* Boston, Little, Brown, 1955.

Stevens, William O. *Washington, the Cinderella city.* New York, Dodd, Mead, 1943.

Thornbrough, Emma Lou. *Booker T. Washington.* Englewood Cliffs, N.J., Prentice-Hall, 1969.

Walker, Anne K. *Tuskegee and the Black Belt.* Richmond, Va., Dietz Press, 1944.

Washington, Booker T. *Education Will Solve the Race Problem. A Reply.* N.Y. Pamphlet. 1900.

———. *The Story of My Life and Work.* Naperville, Ill., J. L. Nichols, 1901.

———. *Tuskegee and Its People: Their Ideals and Achievements.* New York, D. Appleton, 1906.

———. *Up from Slavery.* Garden City, N.Y., Doubleday, 1900.

———. *Working with My Hands.* Garden City, N.Y., Doubleday, Page & Co., 1904.

Who's Who in Colored America. New York, Thomas Yenser, 1933-44.

Institutions Consulted

Booker T. Washington National Monument. United States Department of the Interior. National Park Service. Hardy, Virginia.

Bradford College. Alumni Office. Bradford, Massachusetts.

Columbia University. Alumni Office. New York, New York.

Dallas County Courthouse. Dallas, Texas.

Dallas Public Library. Genealogy Library. History and Social Science Division. Dallas, Texas.

Framingham State College. Framingham, Massachusetts.

Howard University. The Moorland-Spingarn Research Center. Washington, D.C.

Juilliard School. Alumni Office. New York, New York.

Library of Congress. The Booker T. Washington Papers. Washington, D.C.

The New York Public Library. Astor, Lenox and Tilden Foundations. New York, New York.

The Schomburg Center for Research in Black Culture. The New York Public Library. Astor, Lenox and Tilden Foundations. New York, New York.

Tuskegee Institute. Archives. Tuskegee, Alabama.

United States Department of Justice. United States Penitentiary. Leavenworth, Kansas.

Wellesley College. Alumni Office. Wellesley, Massachusetts.

Index

Index

Index

Hall of Fame (N.Y.C.), BTW bust in, 118
Hampton Normal and Agricultural Institute, 11–13, 15, 16, 17, 18, 20, 40, 109, 118
Handy, William C., 111
Hanover, Mass., 22
Harlan, Louis R., xi, 139–40
Harlem Renaissance (N.Y.C.), 98, 99–100
Harrison, Hazel, 106–7, 137
Harrison, Richard B., 111
Harvard University, ix, 21, 49
Haskins, James S., xii
Hathaway, Isaac, 121–22
Hayes, Roland, 111, 112
Heinz, Victor, 106
Hiawatha (Coleridge-Taylor), 58, 59
High Mowing School (Wilton, N.H.), 128
Holt, Nora, 89
Hopedale, Mass., 37
House Un-American Activities Committee, 124
Howard University, 94, 105, 118, 137
Hughes, Langston, 99
Huntington, Collis P., 47
Hurd, Miss (music teacher), 42
Hurston, Zora Neale, 99
Hyde, Elizabeth, 32
Hyde, Ellen, 32

In Dahomey, 70–71
Indians. *See* American Indians
Invisible Man, The, 110

Jamestown, Va., 4; Negro Building (national tercentennial exposition), 80, 90
Jefferson, Margo, xii
Jet magazine, 134
Johnson, Budd, 94
Johnson, J. Rosamond, 70
Johnson, James Weldon, 99
Jordan Marsh Company (Boston, Mass.), 122

Kansas City, Mo., 105, 123, 130, 132–33
Kennedy, Mrs. Alphonso Marcelle, 130. *See also* Pittman, Fannie
Kenny, John A., 88
Kentucky Normal and Industrial Institute, 80

King, Dora S., 22
King, Martin Luther, Jr., 14, 89, 137
Knights of Pythias, 85, 94, 102
Krause, Martin, 53, 62, 63, 64, 68, 69, 75
Ku Klux Klan, 99

Liberia, West Africa, 61, 87
Lincoln Memorial Building Company (Washington, D.C.), 85
Liszt, Franz, x, 62
London, England, PWP in, 56–60, 69–71
Longworth, Alice Roosevelt, 82, 127–28
Lyles, Aubrey, 100

McClendon, Rose, 100
McDuffy, Miss, 108
McKay, Claude, 99
Mackie, Mary F., 11–12
McKinley, William, 47, 81
Malden, W.Va. (BTW birthplace), 6–10, 13; BTW Monument in, 133; Tinkersville community, 8, 9–10, 13
Mandolin Club (Bradford Academy), 44–45
Marrs, S. M. N., 92
Marshall, James Fowle Baldwin, 18
Millender, Lucky, 105
Miller, F. E., 100
Minor, Dan, 94
Mitchell, Abbie, 70–71, 100, 106
Monday, Miss, 122
Montgomery, Ala., 77, 91
Moore, Mary C., 32, 33, 34, 37
Mossell, N. F., 87
Moton, Catherine, 110
Moton, Robert R., 101, 102, 103, 109–10; death of, 112
Murray, Albert, 110

National Association for the Advancement of Colored People (NAACP), x, 51, 98, 99, 124
National Council of Congregational Churches (New Haven, Conn.), 88
National Education Association (NEA), 95–97
National Negro Business League, 1, 80, 84, 88
National Negro Health Week, 88
Negro Business League, 80
Negro Business League Herald, 80
New England, x, 19, 21, 35, 38, 49, 61,

Index

Index

Pittman, William Sidney (husband), x,
72–75, 77–81, 84–86, 100–3, 108–9,
113; birth, background, described,
72–73, 77–80, 84, 85–86, 90, 130;
courtship and marriage to Portia
Washington, x, 72–75, 77–81, 84–86;
death of, 130; end of marriage, 101–3;
failing fortunes of, 84–86, 89–91,
94–95, 100–3
Pond, Miss, 92–94, 104–5
Powell, Adam Clayton, Jr., 14, 124, 125,
126
Preachers, Negro, 14
Price, Sammy, 94
Protestant Episcopal Church
(Framingham, Mass.), 34
Pythian Temple (Dallas, Tex.), 85

Racial problems and conflict, 31–32, 42,
43–44, 59, 82, 93–94, 95, 98–99, 103,
117, 124–25, 129, 136, 137 (see also
specific developments, events, groups,
individuals, places); lynchings and
riots, 98–99, 117; PWP on, 136, 137
Rankin, John, 124–25, 126
Reconstruction era, 14, 26
Rhoads, Joseph J., 91
Rice, Lewis, 8, 11, 14, 17
Roanoke, Va., 120, 122, 124
Robeson, Paul, 87, 100, 112
Rockefeller, John D., ix, 41, 47
Rockefeller Institute (N.Y.C.), 88
Roosevelt, Alice. See Longworth, Alice
Roosevelt
Roosevelt, Franklin D., 108
Roosevelt, Theodore, 53, 58, 81–82, 87,
127–28
Roosevelt, Mrs. Theodore, 82
Roper, Walter Mason, 122
Rosenwald, Julius, 87
Ross, Mary Ann, xi
Ruffner, Lewis, 9, 10, 38
Ruffner, Viola Knapp, 9, 10, 12, 38
Ruffner family, BTW in employ of, 8–10

Schmidt, Henry, 64
School of the Ozarks (Point Lookout,
Mo.), 143
Scotland, PWP in, 70
Scott, Emmett J., 52, 86, 117, 119, 120,
125
Shattuck, Mary, 33
Shepard, Grace F., 33–34, 35

Shuffle Along, 100
Sieveking, Martinus, 105
Silva, Romeo, 130
Sissle, Noble, 100, 111
Slavery (slave era, slave life), 3–5, 6, 7,
14. See also Civil War;
Reconstruction era
Smart, Dorothea L., xi
Smith, Celia (grandmother), 14, 19
Smith, Daniel C., 83
Smith, Fanny Norton. See Washington,
Fanny Norton Smith
"Sometimes I Feel Like a Motherless
Child" (spiritual), 26, 63, 71
Souls of Black Folks, The, 58
Southern Federation of Colored
Women's Clubs, 24
Southern Newspapers Publishers'
Association, 121
Southern Railroad, 32, 37
South to a Very Old Place, 110
Spingarn, Stephen J., 119–20
Spirituals, Negro, 5, 25–26, 35, 39, 41,
60, 62–63, 71, 96–97
Stennis, John C., 136
Stone, Ermine, 92
Stone's (Jesse) Blue Serenaders, Booker
Pittman plays with, 94

Taft, William H., 83
Talley, Professor, 39–40
Taylor, Robert R., 79
Taylor, Robert W., 31–32
Texas Association of Negro Musicians,
92
There Is Confusion, 99
Thrasher, Max Bennett, 86
Togoland (later Togo), 40, 66
Toomer, Jean, 99
Trotter, William Monroe, 49, 50–51, 87,
111
Truman, Harry, 120
Tuck, William M., 123
Tuskegee, Ala., PWP born in, 1
Tuskegee Alumni Club (Washington,
D.C.), 140
Tuskegee and Its People, 39
Tuskegee Institute, ix, 1, 32, 34–35, 36,
37, 38, 41, 43, 46–47, 55, 56, 59, 71,
72, 77, 78, 80, 87–88, 89, 91, 109–14
134, 135, 136; and BTW Memorial,
115–16, 118, 125; end of PWP's
official connection with, 109–14; John

Index

A. Andrew Memorial Hospital, 88; PWP at, 25ff., 38–41, 42–43, 46–47, 101ff.; PWP returns to teach at, 101ff.; School of Music established in, 103; start and growth of, BTW and, 15ff. (*see also* Washington, Booker T.)

Tuskegee Normal School for Colored Youth, 1, 15–29 (*see also* Tuskegee Institute); start and growth of, 15ff.

Ulrich affair, BTW and, 82–84
Uncle Tom's Cabin, 44
United Negro College Fund, 118
Unwin, Mr. and Mrs. T. Fisher, 57, 70
Up from Slavery, 5, 40, 86, 135, 139

Victoria, Queen, 57
Virginia General Assembly, and BTW Memorial, 118, 119

Wales, Prince and Princess of, 56, 71
Walker, A'Lelia, 100
Walker, Madam C. J., 100
Walker, George, 57
Wallace, George, 136
Wall Street Journal, 143
Walters, Bishop Alexander, 87
Washington, Amanda (aunt), 2, 6, 13, 21
Washington, Booker, III (nephew), 108, 117, 119
Washington, Booker T. (father), ix, 92, 98, 100, 101, 109, 113, 128, 129, 139, 140, 141; Atlanta speech by, xi, 27–29, 41, 135, 136; autobiography, *Up From Slavery,* 5, 40, 86, 135, 139; birth, childhood, education, family, 2–13; books and writings, 86; commemorative coin in honor of, 119–23; commemorative stamp in honor of, 112, 127, 129; criticism and controversy surrounding philosophy and doctrine of, ix–x, 2, 28, 39, 44, 49–52, 82–84, 87, 89, 98–99, 109, 121, 134–35, 136–37, 138, 141; and daily life, and routine at Tuskegee, 46–47; and daughter's marriage to Sidney Pittman, 73, 74, 75, 77–78, 80, 81, 84–85, 86; and daughter's stay in Europe, 53–69 *passim,* 71–72; and daughter's study of German, 40–41; death of first wife and remarriage, 19–21; death and funeral of, 88–89;

death of second wife and remarriage, 21–24; described, career and influence of, 1ff., 43, 48, 87 (*see also* specific developments, events, individuals); and doctrine and philosophy of social separation and race uplift through dignity of labor, ix–x, 16, 28–29, 41, 49, 50–52, 58–59, 82–84, 87, 89, 143; marriage to Fanny Norton Smith, his first wife and PWP's mother, 13–14, 17–19; origin of name, 2; posthumous honors and Memorials to, 112, 114, 115–30, 133; relationship with his daughter, 19–20 (*see also under* Pittman, Portia Marshall Washington); as spokesman and leader of his race, 26, 28–29, 81–82, 83–84, 86–89, 128; statue at Tuskegee of, 91; as a student at Hampton Institute, 11–13; teaches at Hampton Institute, 15; and Tuskegee Institute, 1, 15ff., 34–37, 41 (*see also* Tuskegee Institute); and Ulrich affair, 82–84

Washington, Booker T. II, (brother) 20, 21, 107–8

Washington, D.C. (District of Columbia), 14–15, 36–37, 79, 80, 85, 105, 123, 129, 132–33, 134, 140

Washington, Ernest Davidson (brother), 20, 21, 70, 107

Washington, Fanny Norton Smith (mother), 13–14, 15, 17–19, 129, 139; death of 18–19; marriage, described, 17–18

Washington, Gloria Davidson (niece), 118

Washington, Jane (grandmother), 2, 3, 6–8, 11; death of, 13

Washington, John (uncle), 2, 7, 11, 13, 22

Washington, Margaret James Murray ("Maggie," the third Mrs. Booker T. Washington, PWP's second stepmother), 23–24, 25, 27, 29, 36, 38, 39, 42, 45–46, 68, 74; an BTW's death, 89; death of, 91; and PWP's marriage to Sidney Pittman, 74, 75, 80; *Tuskegee and Its People* by, 39

Washington, Olivia A. Davidson (the second Mrs. Booker T. Washington, PWP's first stepmother), 19, 20–21, 29, 31, 32, 35, 38

Index

Washington, Portia Marshall. *See* Pittman, Portia Washington Marshall

Waters, Ethel, 100

Wayland Seminary, BTW attends, 14–15

Wellesley College (Mass.), 41–42, 43, 49

West Virginia, 9. *See also* specific places

Weymouth, Mass., 37, 48

White, Clarence Cameron, 81

Williams, Burt, 57

Williams, Daniel T., xi

Wood, Charles Winter, 113–14

World War I, 99, 117

World War II, 111, 117

S4

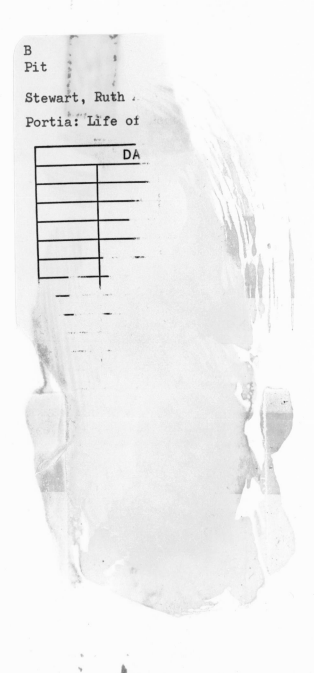

B
Pit

Stewart, Ruth

Portia: Life of

DA